PRIVATISATION

...FAIR SHARES FOR ALL OR SELLING THE FAMILY SILVER?

DAYS OF DECISION
Series Editor: Julia Neuberger

PRIVATISATION
...FAIR SHARES FOR ALL OR SELLING THE FAMILY SILVER?

PAPERMAC

First published 1987 by
PAPERMAC
a division of Macmillan Publishers Limited
4 Little Essex Street London WC2R 3LF
and Basingstoke
Associated companies in Auckland, Delhi, Dublin, Gaborone,
Hamburg, Harare, Hong Kong, Johannesburg, Kuala Lumpur,
Lagos, Manzini, Melbourne, Mexico City, Nairobi, New York,
Singapore and Tokyo

British Library Cataloguing in Publication Data
Julia Neuberger
    Privatisation: fair shares for all or
    selling the family silver? — (Days of
    decision). —— (Papermac).
    1. Privatisation —— Great Britain
    I. Title II. Rentoul, John III. Ezra,   Sir Derek
    IV. Clarke, Peter V. Series
    338.0941   HD4148

ISBN 0–333–44770–1

Typeset by Columns of Reading
Printed by Richard Clay plc, Bungay, Suffolk

Contents

Introduction

One of the major priorities of Conservative policy since 1983 has been the privatisation of nationalised industries, along with the contracting-out of NHS and local authority services to private companies. Conservatives see privatisation as a way of encouraging efficiency, limiting the power of trade unions, breaking up the vast empires of the national industries into smaller, more locally responsive units, and running industry for the benefit of share-holders and consumers rather than the workforce.

Resistance to this policy has been most marked from trade unions and local authorities, including some Conservative-led authorities who feel that the Government is doctrinaire on this issue. Yet it has been generally supported by the City's financial institutions, by a considerable section of the public, whose response to British Telecom and British Gas shares has been enthusiastic, and by economists and finance experts, who argue that the increased efficiency will be of benefit to everyone. Meanwhile there are many who do not wholly agree with either side. They believe the nationalised industries, the local authorities and the NHS services are capable of efficiency, if they are given the freedom to achieve it and if they are properly run. They also see the root causes of many of these inefficiencies in bad management, poor industrial relations, overt and constant central government intervention and lack of proper trade union legislation. The committed opponents of privatisation share some of these feelings, as well as a belief in the inherent value in keeping specific services and industries in public ownership.

The history of the debate itself is fascinating, as is the change in vocabulary from denationalisation to privatisation. The question of who should run and own our industries and social services is one of the key issues of the late 1980s, and this book will help the reader to decide for him or herself whether privatisation means fair shares for all or if it is merely the alibi of a government desperately selling off the family silver.

Julia Neuberger

Privatisation: The Case Against

John Rentoul

Introduction: Claims and Counter-Claims

The leader of Albania, Enver Hoxha, warned before his death in 1985 that departures from the true path of Stalinism would end up as a 'bucket of crabs'. If only someone had given a similar warning to Mrs Thatcher eight years ago about the dangers of departing from the equally unpopular legacy of Wilson, Heath and Callaghan. Mikhail Gorbachev has made quite a name for himself by ignoring Hoxha's advice and rejecting the USSR's equivalent of the post-war consensus; but rejecting such a consensus in Britain has driven us to the market, to sell up and fire the servants. It has driven us to privatisation: to a bucket of crabs.

Privatisation is a word which was first taken out of quotation marks in Britain in 1980, initially by opponents of the Government, especially trade unionists. It referred to the turning of public services over to private contractors; it was a derogatory term, an irregular construction with connotations of privateering, or of wicked capitalists exploiting cheap labour for private gain from the exchequer. The word was extended to include the selling-off of public corporations, a policy which got on to television news in 1982 and for which there was no existing convenient word. Both policies are inspired by the same philosophy, which holds that it is always best to leave decisions to private individuals acting collectively through the mechanism of the market.

Privatisation can be assessed at several levels. What, first, of the 'hard' left-wing case: that privatisation is a vicious attack

on democratic trade unions by an ideological Tory Government which is stuffing the pockets of its capitalist supporters
by legalising the exploitation of ordinary working people and
especially low-paid women and black workers? As an explana-
tion of privatisation, it is internally consistent and sufficient.
It accords with the facts. Phrased less emotively, it would be
adequate to explain privatisation – both denationalisation
and contracting-out – to a party of visiting Martians. They
could understand privatisation as a measure designed to
strengthen organised capital and to weaken organised labour;
or, in party political terms, to enrich the financers, friends and
supporters of the Conservative Party and impoverish the trade
unions who finance the Conservatives' main political
opposition.

But while the hard-left case is logically sufficient to explain
privatisation, it cannot be the whole story. It is safe to say that
privatisation is not generally perceived in quite this light. The
Conservative arguments for privatisation must be credible
enough to stave off the wholly uncharitable interpretation.

The Conservative argument is primarily one of efficiency.
'The reduction of waste, bureaucracy and over-government
will yield substantial savings . . . local direct labour schemes
waste an estimated £400 million a year,' said the Conservative Manifesto in 1979, referring – obscurely and without
evidence – to directly employed council manual workers.

Conservatives argue that subjecting public-sector activities
to market forces makes them more efficient; this enables them
to compete with other countries, reduces public spending and
frees resources to be used elsewhere. Advocates of privatisation accept parts of the hard-left case, although a slightly
different gloss is put on them. Privatisation is designed to
weaken trade unions, Conservatives say; trade unions in the
public sector were too powerful, and have been shielded from
the economic realities of the market by taxpayers' money.
Privatisation usefully exposes unions to the pressure of
market forces.

Many Tories will also happily admit that privatisation is
designed to create support for the Conservative Party. Wider

share ownership creates a larger class of people who have a self-interest in maintaining a Conservative Government. This is not 'buying votes', say Conservatives; it is helping to create a more responsible political climate. If this is to the advantage of the Tory party, that is because it is the only truly responsible political party. Wider share ownership, argue the Conservatives, brings wider understanding of the economic reality of what an excellent thing profit is, and enables the working class to see that now we are all capitalists, if not actually all members of the Conservative Party.

Some supporters of privatisation allege that it 'spreads' wealth more widely, allowing previously hard-done-by workers an opportunity to share in the ownership of the nation's productive assets, although some proponents of this argument do not necessarily promote the Government's cause. David Massingham, for instance, wrote to the *Guardian* (3 October 1986):

> My enjoyment of the prospect of spending some of the profits of my speculation in TSB shares was greatly enhanced when I read the sanctimonious whingeing of several of your correspondents.
>
> It is always amusing when those who lack either the wit or the ability to benefit from such opportunities seek to vent their frustration and envy by vilifying the supposed greed of others, while advancing apparent concern for the welfare of the disadvantaged.
>
> The truth is that many of those who will profit from the sale of the TSB will be first-time buyers of shares, who will have worked long years for scant rewards.

Less *outré* Conservatives argue more soberly that it is worth selling off public corporations at a discount, because it provides an extra incentive to join the share-owning classes, which ultimately redounds to the greater good of the nation. This is quite a proper argument, although one may disagree with it. Politicians of all parties are always in favour of subsidies for certain forms of civic behaviour they consider to be virtuous. (Some right-wing theoreticians may be against all subsidies in principle – Nigel Lawson probably was once – but practical politicians in power tend to hold slightly different views.) The Labour-controlled Greater London Council – on a relatively modest scale – subsidised worker co-ops and facilities for disadvantaged groups. Liberal and SDP politicians believe in public subsidies for regional investment. Conservatives believe in subsidies to encourage people to become shareholders.

The fact that these subsidies are overwhelmingly taken up by the already prosperous, not to mention syndicates of even more prosperous City stags, is, to the average Conservative, merely a matter of left-wing sour grapes. The subsidising of mortgage interest does not greatly trouble Norman Tebbit's conscience either. The benefit to the whole nation of wider share and home ownership is believed to outweigh any such difficulties.

There are intangible aspects to this benefit. Property owners are thought to be more responsible, more independent of the State and more accepting of the advantages of individual pursuit of profit. But leaving aside those intangible benefits for the moment, the Conservative case for privatisation can be reduced to three main propositions, which are either true or not.

One, that *privatisation increases efficiency*. Not only that, but that in public enterprises it is usually the best way of increasing efficiency.

Two, that *assets sales spread wealth more widely*, and give more 'power to the people'.

Three, that *whoever benefits or loses from privatisation in the short term, everyone is better off in the long run*; meaning that the more that is left to 'market forces' and the less to Government, the stronger the economy will be in world markets, which is the only way to secure long-term prosperity for all.

All these statements are capable of proof, so let us investigate them. What are the effects of privatisation?

There have so far been three distinct types of privatisation: selling off human assets, that is, public services, and selling off two kinds of capital assets: council houses and public corporations. Selling off council houses was the first phase, taking place mostly during Mrs Thatcher's first term. Much of the Government action to promote contracting-out also occurred between 1979 and 1983, although the effects have been more gradual. Selling public corporations became a prominent part of Conservative Party policy almost accidentally, but as a logical consequence of earlier developments, towards the end of Mrs Thatcher's first term of office, and was put into practice mainly during the second term.

Let us examine each type of privatisation and test the Government's claims for each of them.

Selling Council Houses

The sale of council houses was one of the more specific and popular of the Conservatives' 1979 election promises. Since then over one million homes have been sold at discounts of at least one-third; sales peaked in 1982 at 222,000, and were down to 109,000 in 1985. In 1986 the Government introduced new measures to keep up the momentum, increasing the maximum discount from £25,000 to £35,000, increasing the discounts on flats to a minimum of 44 per cent after two years' tenure and a maximum of 70 per cent after fifteen years (on houses the discounts range from 32 per cent to 60 per cent after thirty years), and making it easier to buy council flats by laying down in law how councils must calculate service charges for privatised flats in mixed blocks.

Has this led to greater 'efficiency'? Well, there are two kinds of efficiency in housing: one is to do with repairs, and the other is the efficiency with which housing is allocated to those who want or need it, which I shall consider later. If individual householders have the resources, they will generally be able to get repairs done more satisfactorily themselves than if they have to report them to the local council. But remember that 'if': while most people who buy their council houses *do* have the resources to be able to pay for their own repairs, not everyone does. What is more, the main exception to the efficiency rule is blocks of flats, where some form of collective organisation is needed for major repairs; and some of the worst stories of incompetence, delay and shoddy work come from the private sector. Most owners of leasehold flats would probably rather have the local council as the freeholder than a private company or individual. The best arrangement is usually for the leaseholders themselves to share the ownership of the freehold of their block. So privatising council houses may increase efficiency, but privatising council flats, in itself, is unlikely to do so.

Do council house sales spread wealth? The effect of council house sales has been to increase the proportion of the population who own their own home. Since 1979, the proportion of the adult population owning or part-owning their home has risen from 50 per cent to 56 per cent.* About three-quarters of that increase was due to council tenants buying their homes. Even the Labour Party has belatedly decided that this is a good thing, but it is what I call 'divisive egalitarianism'. Because home-ownership is the largest single form of personal wealth in this country, extending it adds to the number of people who have a significant store of wealth – even if it cannot be readily cashed – and who have

---

* I have calculated this figure from the *General Household Survey*, and discuss it further in my forthcoming book, *The Rich Get Richer: the growth of inequality in Britain in the 1980s*, to be published by Pluto Press/Allison and Busby. A lot of rubbish is talked about the number of people who are home-owners in Britain today, some of it by Conservative ministers. It is *not* the case that two-thirds of the British population own their own home. About 60 per cent of the homes in the UK are owner-occupied, which is something slightly different, because some of the adults who live in them are not the owners, or even part-owners. The 63 per cent figure which is often carelessly referred to is the percentage of owner-occupied homes in England, but as the equivalent figure in Scotland is only 40 per cent, the national average is only 60 per cent.

access to the freedoms of the property market. So selling council houses does spread wealth more widely, but it also deepens the divide between home-owners and council tenants, because those who are left behind on the wrong side of the divide are worse off.

The third claim – that in the end everyone benefits from council house sales – is demonstrably false. The rise in home-ownership can't be separated from what is happening at the same time to the 44 per cent of people who are *not* home-owners. They have been treated in much the same way as Marie Antionette treated the starving Parisians: 'Let them buy houses.' Many council tenants cannot afford to buy their homes, almost regardless of the size of discount the Government is prepared to force local councils to give. The average amount paid by tenants for their home was £13,800 in September 1986, and that was with an average discount of nearly half (46 per cent). Similarly, looking at the housing market as a whole, many people in private rented housing cannot afford high house prices on high mortgage rates, especially since 'mortgage rates have risen steeply because of the Government's financial mismanagement'.*

The fact that tenants often cannot afford to buy would not matter so much if council housing or private rented accommodation were a desirable alternative to home-ownership. Of course, neither of them currently is, and this is also largely the Government's responsibility. One of its most dogmatic acts has been to prevent local councils from spending the money they receive from council house sales, a rule which is a part of 'privatisation' insofar as the word means the worship of the private and denigration of the public, in whatever context. Councils are only allowed to spend one-fifth of their receipts; the other four-fifths has, in effect, to go towards the reduction of borrowing (the motive behind the rule being the Government's hostility on ideological grounds to public-sector borrowing of any sort).

* The Conservative Manifesto, 1979.

The effect of council house sales, like that of selling public corporations, is to reduce the assets owned by public authorities on behalf of us all, and to transfer them to selected private individuals, who pay for them, but at a special bargain price. In principle, this is not necessarily unfair. If the discount – the element of public subsidy – were reasonable and the manner of selecting the private beneficiaries fair, then the important question would be: what is done with the money received in payment for these public assets?

Given that most of the beneficiaries of council house sales are not rich – certainly not as rich as most of the beneficiaries of the South-east's house price boom – it would seem quite egalitarian that they should buy their homes at a discount, provided that such a discount were made up to local councils by Central Government, and provided that the money were spent on building new council houses, or making old ones fit for human habitation.

Far from preventing councils from spending most of the money they receive from house sales, councils should be required by law to spend the money on replacing the housing stock. Otherwise privatising council houses has the effect of reducing the amount and quality of accommodation with which councils have to fulfil their legal obligation to put roofs over the heads of the homeless.

Most people do want to own their own homes, and local councils could then become the means by which those who cannot afford to buy could be given access to the property market on the basis of need.

But the Government's policy of council house sales is, in effect, one of giving to the poor by stealing from the very poor. The collective assets owned by local councils on behalf of all the people, with the intention of benefiting them according to housing need, are being reduced.

Contracting-out

In February 1987, Environment Secretary Nicholas Ridley announced the 'postponement' of new laws to force local councils to put refuse collection, street and public building cleaning, catering, school meals, vehicle maintenance and park-keeping out to tender.

A few councils have, of course, experimented with contracting-out, especially refuse collection, without being required to do so. The problems they encountered led to a Conservative Government appointing a committee to look into the question. It concluded that in the interests of efficiency and public health, 'local authorities should not employ contractors to collect household refuse'. But that, unfortunately, was the conclusion of a Committee of Inquiry appointed by Sir Alec Douglas-Home in 1963.*

Nor, even then, were the perils of contracting-out a new discovery. In what should really have been the last word on the subject, the former chief executive of the local council in Kensington said:

> If there was one description of work which should be undertaken by local authorities, it was that of the collection and disposal of house refuse. It was in the interests of the contractors to do as little as possible, and so increase their profits.†

That happened in 1897. But some values are obviously more Victorian than others.

After the unsuccessful experiments with refuse collection in the 1950s, local councils tended not to try contracting-out new services. In the early 1970s some 40–50 per cent of

---

* *Refuse Storage and Collection*, Department of the Environment, 1967.
† *Local Services: The Case Against Privatisation*, National Union of Public Employees, p. 7.

architectural services, for instance, were put out to the private sector; by 1980 less than 20 per cent was contracted-out.* By 1981 only two councils in the whole country used private contractors for refuse collection: Maldon and Mid-Bedfordshire. The use of contractors in the National Health Service also declined. Between 1965 and 1984, the number of private catering contracts in the NHS dropped from 33 to two (sic).† Those two contracts accounted for one-fifth of one per cent of all NHS spending on catering.

In the National Health Service, and for most council services, the new Conservative Government in 1979 relied at first on persuasion. But, despite Health Minister Gerard Vaughan's best efforts to persuade health authorities that contracting-out 'can be an excellent way of increasing efficiency, thus freeing money for patient care',‡ the NHS went on cancelling contracts and deciding to do the work itself. In the first four years of Mrs Thatcher's Government, 1979 to 1983, the percentage of NHS spending on cleaning that went to private contractors fell from 2.4 per cent to 2 per cent. Only in laundry services was a significant proportion of NHS spending contracted-out, and that proportion fell from 14.7 per cent in 1979 to 11.5 per cent in 1983.

In September 1983, a month before Mrs Thatcher famously announced to the Conservative Party conference that 'the NHS is safe with us', Health and Social Services Secretary Norman Fowler decided that where reasoned argument had failed, bludgeon would enable health authorities to discover the true path. He issued a circular which 'instructed' health authorities to put all hospital cleaning, catering and laundry services out to tender by late 1986. The existing work-force would have to bid against private firms for their work.

This was despite near-unanimous opposition to the idea from health authorities when the idea was first formally

---

* Department of the Environment Green Paper, *Competition in the Provision of Local Authority Services*, February 1985, para 52.
† *Local Services*, p. 7.
‡ Circular to authorities, August 1981.

proposed in February 1983. NHS Unlimited, a campaign against private medicine, has published a huge selection of hostile comments from regional and district health authorities.* Sixty-eight health authorities are quoted, mostly pointing out in one way or another that the present low level of contracting-out in the NHS did not come about by accident, but because over the years contracting-out had been tried and direct labour found to be more satisfactory. The management team at Worcester District Health Authority, for example, wrote:

> Contract domestic services were used at the three Wychavon Health Centres until 1980. Over time complaints were received about poor standards, and there were considerable problems with supervision. Although the service was cheaper initially, this also ceased to be true. For that reason the service was discontinued and since then in-house staff have been used to everyone's satisfaction.

Some health authorities told the minister to get lost, saying they had no intention of acting on his circular. East Dyfed adopted the most lofty tone:

> It is the Authority's policy that all ward-based staff or staff providing services in in-patient areas must be employed by and, therefore, be under the direct control of the Health Authority. The Authority regards this as a cornerstone of its duty to provide and maintain acceptable levels of care provided by individuals of an appropriate standard of probity and personal integrity.

Central Government does not have absolute control over local health authorities, but Norman Fowler tightened his grip with the gradual replacement of reluctant members, using his power of not renewing the appointments of chairs and some

---

* 'The Health Authority View', Memorandum 7, November 1984.

members. Some authorities are still defying the policy. Some have complied, sometimes being unable to attract tenders and often awarding the contract to the existing work-force. Others have delayed, and allowed their timetable for tendering to fall behind.

Soon after coming to power, Mrs Thatcher's Government made it compulsory for local councils to put building and road works out to competitive tender and, if councils' direct labour organisations kept the work, then they would have to earn a 5 per cent 'profit' (Local Government Planning and Land Act 1980). Quite a lot of this kind of heavy construction and maintenance work was already contracted-out, but the new law did change the attitudes of managers of many direct labour organisations. This was not because of the need to make a profit, according to the Association of Direct Labour Organisations, but because of 'exposure to the idea that output is valued rather than costed. Under the [new] rules, work is paid for only on the basis of an assessment of its value. Under the traditional system, work is paid for on the basis of what it costs. It is this which is the motor for changes in culture.'*

For other council services, however, the Government relied on persuasion, and was only marginally more successful – although not with Labour-controlled councils – than in the NHS. By March 1986 only twenty-four councils had awarded refuse collection contracts to the private sector, and five more had contracted-out street cleaning. A further twenty-six had put refuse collection or street cleaning contracts out to tender, but the existing work-force kept the work.† After an initial burst of enthusiasm, the *Local Government Chronicle*, which conducts an annual survey of new private contracts, reported in June 1984 that 'the number of authorities actively pursuing privatisation [of any services] has dwindled'. (In April 1985, it

---

* Norman Flynn and Kieron Walsh, *Managing to Survive*, Association of Direct Labour Organisations, Bathgate, 1986, p. 18.
† Figures from BFI-Wastecare quoted by Domberger, Meadowcroft and Thompson, 'Competitive Tendering and Efficiency', *Fiscal Studies*, November 1986.

said that 'only a handful of local authorities have privatised services in the last year'. In 1986 it came to the same conclusion.)

So, in February 1985 the Government published a Green Paper proposing to force councils to put five other areas of service, apart from building and roads, out to competitive tender: refuse collection, public building and street cleaning, vehicle maintenance, maintenance of playing fields and parks, and catering. 'Far too many authorities appear to have been unwilling to open services to competition,' the Green Paper declared. It was not well received, even by Conservative councils. The Association of County Councils, which then had a majority of Tory members, said: 'The Association regards the degree of compulsion proposed as objectionable in principle. . . . Over-emphasis on competition could have the effect of increasing costs while actually reducing efficiency.'

The Tory-controlled Association of District Councils was similarly unimpressed:

> Compulsion is not only unnecessary and counter-productive but will further undermine democratic accountability for local services. . . .
> 　The proposals to extend tendering, accounting and reporting requirements to other services will significantly increase manpower and costs.

Individual Conservative councils were more outspoken. Rossendale Borough Council was 'concerned at the threat of privatisation of the services which this council provides, along with the insecurity this action will bring', and promised to 'strive to safeguard those services'. But perhaps the political damage had already been done. Rossendale is Tory-controlled no more: the electors have given their verdict.

Individual Conservative councillors were even more outspoken. John Jenner, vice-chair of the Policy Committee on Weymouth and Portland council said,

> The Government's intentions are so serious as to virtually crucify local authorities and all the things I have stood

for over the past twenty-five years. . . . If you are going to agree to this lot you may as well resign from the council now.*

Whether this hail of protests had an effect on the Government or not, nothing more was heard of the Green Paper for over a year. But in the 1986 Queen's Speech the Government announced its intention to bring legislation forward. Environment Secretary Nicholas Ridley emphasised the electioneering aspect of the Green Paper, the proposal to ban 'political' clauses in public-sector contracts. But within a few months, in February 1987, electioneering had got so out of hand that the parliamentary timetable had to be cleared and Ridley put off the new legislation effectively until after the election.

Has contracting-out, where it has occurred, achieved greater efficiency? The Trades Union Congress has published two dossiers called *Contractors' Failures* (1984) and *More Contractors' Failures* (1986), which make racy reading in a modern Dickensian fashion, although, like Dickens, they become rather repetitive. Of course, they are wholly biased against private contractors in that they list only the failures. Many contractors run acceptable or good services most of the time. But conversely, the TUC dossiers are just a tiny selection of the worst incidents and cases in local councils and health authorities.

The drawback to the TUC's approach is that it is anecdotal evidence. It may be true that, for example, Office Cleaning Services once left blood on the floor of an operating theatre in Addenbrookes hospital in Cambridge, but that does not necessarily disprove the assertion that contracting-out is *generally* more efficient than direct labour at delivering a comparable standard of service.†

The truth of this assertion can only be tested by measuring

---

* *Local Services*, p. 24.
† *Cambridge Evening News*, 1 April 1985, quoted in *Labour Research*, May 1985.

and comparing the performance and cost of services carried out by private contractors and by direct employees, adjusting as far as possible for different circumstances. This has never been done; but the closest to it was a study carried out in 1986 by the Institute for Fiscal Studies which looked at refuse collection.*

The study used a technique called regression analysis to examine data from 305 local councils between 1983 and 1985, including nineteen which used private contractors and another ten who had put their refuse collection out to tender, but who had retained the service in-house. It found that private contractors were 22 per cent cheaper than direct labour, and that direct labour which had gone through the tendering process was 17 per cent cheaper than direct labour which had not been exposed to the cold winds of market competition.

The Institute's analysis adjusted for almost every variable you could think of – density of houses, reclaimed paper, bottle-banks – and some you couldn't – including an adjustment for the presence of heteroskedasticity (sic). On the question of the standard of service, however, the study only dealt with the method and frequency of collection, and referred readers to a different piece of research, a detailed case-study of five local councils that had privatised their refuse collection. This researcher concluded that the councils which had awarded private contracts

> consider that they have continued to receive the same standard of service required at a lower cost than they were facing before. [And] the penalty clauses for non-performance built into the contract were considered sufficient to ensure the required standard of service.

This is hardly decisive, objective evidence; it is the subjective opinion of the officers (presumably) of councils which have decided to contract out. They are not likely to tell an academic researcher that they think the penalty clauses are insufficient

---

* Domberger, Meadowcroft and Thompson, *Fiscal Studies*, November 1986.

to ensure what they were designed to do.

Nevertheless, a 22 per cent saving is a big one, and I would not argue that the standards of private contractors are generally a full 22 per cent worse than those of direct labour organisations. As the Institute for Fiscal Studies points out, 'a contract can be specified for refuse collection in which the expected outputs are measurable and in which monitoring of compliance is comparatively straightforward'. In other words, it is not actually beyond the wit of council officials to specify and monitor standards, which is something they have to do with a direct labour force in any case. And any slight change in the unmeasurable 'quality' of the service is hardly likely to be worth paying so much extra for.

But the Institute's study ignores another critical variable: the pay and conditions of the workforce. Part of the 22 per cent reduction in cost has been achieved by contractors paying their work-forces less than the council's employees. The Institute's researchers may regard wage cuts as increased 'efficiency'. Most people would not. The smaller 17 per cent saving by direct labour forces which had been forced to compete with the private sector suggests that contractors could be paying their workers at least 5 per cent less. This is because council employees are covered by national pay agreements, which would make it difficult to cut their pay: the councils' 17 per cent saving could be mostly 'genuine', allowing for a reduction in service quality. So it appears that privatisation, or the threat of privatisation, can increase efficiency. As the Institute concluded: 'It is the introduction of competition, rather than awarding contracts to private firms, which is the critical factor.' It also, however, encourages wage-cutting, and may reduce standards. 'Standards' in many public services means the quality of care.

Market forces may be very good at, for example, deciding what colour shirts people prefer or what record ought to be Number One, but they are not good at caring for people. To cite just one of the TUC's case studies: Crothalls, a subsidiary of Pritchards, was fined £9,000 for failing to meet cleanliness standards in its contract for cleaning Croydon health centres and clinics in 1985. A report on Crothall's performance by the health authority general manager, obtained by the *Guardian*, described 'stained lavatories, dirty surgeries, and potentially dangerous security lapses'. A senior health authority official was quoted as being 'extremely angry' at the 'appalling' standards since Crothalls had taken over from NHS cleaners six months before.

The assumption behind the Government's claim to increase efficiency, of course, is that efficiency is a good thing. But efficiency means producing the same output with fewer resources, or more output with the same resources: so far, privatisation has meant producing a similar level of output – that is service – with fewer resources, which mainly consist of labour. So greater efficiency, in the context of privatisation to date, means greater unemployment.

In times of fuller employment, it might have been possible to consider efficiency in a narrow sense, simply looking at one task and asking 'how can we do this using the fewest resources?' But in times of high unemployment, there are significant hidden costs in job losses. Surely these should be part of any sensible definition of efficiency? If they are, then the Government should perhaps look at efficiency the other way round: in terms of maximising output instead of minimising costs. Greater efficiency could be to provide a better street cleaning service, or better NHS catering, or better school meals, with the same number of workers at the same level of pay.

The Conservative Government's policy, however, does not even try to isolate increased productivity and better work organisation, which are the elements of what most people would think of as greater 'efficiency': it *also* explicitly tries to force wages down, because it believes in lower wages for their own sake.

This is part of the third claim for privatisation made by the Government: that although the existing work-force may lose out through job losses and lower wages, we all benefit in the end. I shall come back to job losses later, but how does the argument in favour of lower wages work?

Some contractors are keen to distinguish between 'efficiency' and 'lower wages'. Mr R. T. Cresswell, Technical Director of Exclusive Cleansing Services, attacked its competitors, Taskmasters and Pritchards, on their street-cleaning services for

> using inadequate numbers of people, paying the lowest possible rates of pay, giving poor conditions of service (e.g. no pension benefits), using old vehicles maintained to minimum standards, and generally keeping costs at an absolutely rock-bottom level.

He contrasted it with Exclusive's policy, which is 'to offer reasonable terms and conditions [and] to foster good staff relationships' (letter to City of Gloucester, 31 August 1983).

It sounds like a good policy, but in February 1985 *Health Service Journal* reported that children under sixteen had been employed by Exclusive on its cleaning contract at Wokingham Hospital in Berkshire, in contravention of the terms of its agreement with the hospital. Jack Broadley, Exclusive's managing director, said that three girls under sixteen had been employed doing washing up for less than eight hours a week, and that they had the necessary work permits. Exclusive had won the contract with a bid that was barely half the next lowest tender, and had problems recruiting staff because they cut wages from £2.15 to £1.72 per hour when they took over.*

The danger of contractors exploiting low-paid workers to undercut their competitors for public-sector contracts was recognised by Lord Salisbury's Conservative Government in 1891. With the support of Gladstone's Liberal opposition, it passed a Fair Wages Resolution, which aimed to stop employers cutting their workers' wages or increasing their hours in order to compete for Government contracts. The resolution was amended by Asquith's Liberal Government in 1909 to define 'fair wages' as those agreed between trade

---

* *Public Service Action* No. 14, 1985.

unions and employers. A new Fair Wages Resolution was passed by the House of Commons in 1946, which laid down that 'the contractor shall recognise the freedom of his work-people to be members of trade unions', and that the contractor should pay wages at least as good as those agreed through collective bargaining, or the 'general level' in similar industries. It stipulated that disputes about 'fair wages' should be referred to an independent tribunal, latterly the Central Arbitration Committee.

Only really dedicated free-marketeers could think that the public sector should use its purchasing power to encourage the payment of 'unfair wages'. Norman Tebbit is such a person. In 1983, when he was Employment Minister, he abolished the Fair Wages Resolution.

The reasons his department gave for abolishing the Resolution were that it had fallen into disuse, and that 'nearly all recent claims have been made not by employees who are low paid by any objective standard, but by trade unions on behalf of relatively high paid members'. If it had fallen into disuse (which it hadn't: there were fifty claims in 1981, and it had a deterrent effect), then why bother to abolish it? As for the second reason, the last claim under the resolution to be decided by the Central Arbitration Committee was on behalf of privatised refuse collectors working for Grandmet in Wandsworth. In June 1983 the Committee found that £109 a week for a collector was 'unfair' and ordered Grandmet to pay a rise of £6 a week, and to cut working hours from forty to thirty-nine hours a week. It also ordered an £8-a-week rise for chargehand/drivers on top of their £115 a week.

The Fair Wages Resolution had been written into all Central Government, local council and NHS contracts, and some health authorities simply replaced it with a new clause of their own. This was not what Norman Tebbit had in mind, as Health Minister Kenneth Clarke made plain to health authorities in a circular in 1984:

> Some districts are seeking to require contractors who tender for NHS support services to employ staff on

Whitley [that is, nationally negotiated] terms and conditions of service. . . . This is unacceptable to ministers. . . . We consider that it is quite wrong for authorities [to] specify the terms and conditions for service which private contractors should provide for staff working on NHS contracts. There is no sensible basis upon which a health authority can interfere in this way in the relationship between the contractor and its employees.*

Kenneth Clarke was even prepared to interfere, presumably on a sensible basis, to stop Norwich District Health Authority giving a cleaning contract to its own staff in 1985. The in-house tender was more expensive than private contractors' bids, but it preserved pay and conditions; the authority was instructed to think again. It still awarded the contract to the in-house staff, but made cuts in cleaning hours.

The abolition of the Fair Wages Resolution is more significant in the context of the NHS than in Local Government, because the work that is contracted-out in the health service, mostly cleaning and catering, is overwhelmingly done by women working part-time. These workers tend not to be unionised, unlike full-time male refuse collectors or street cleaners, and are most vulnerable to downward pressure on their pay and conditions.

There is almost no official information on the pay of part-time contract cleaners, most of whom are employed for fewer than sixteen hours a week, to avoid providing the benefits of the Employment Protection Act, and paid less than £39 a week, to avoid paying National Insurance contributions. As a result, cleaners are not entitled to sick pay or the higher State pension (SERPS).

Surveys carried out by the trade union research body, Labour Research, show hourly pay rates for part-time contract cleaners of between £1.46 and £1.96, although rates higher

---

* Quoted by Angela Coyle, *Dirty Business*, West Midlands Low Pay Unit 1986, p. 16.

than £1.70 tend to be paid only when workers are unionised.*
The West Midlands Low Pay Unit reports that 'in inner-city
areas, contractors have little problem in recruiting labour at
£1.40 an hour'.†

Angela Coyle, in her study of women and trade union
organisation in contract cleaning, *Dirty Business*, points out
that women do not choose to be low-paid cleaners, but it fits
into a day which is cut up by family responsibilities and
unpaid work. She quotes one cleaner:

> Before I got this job I worked in a factory. I packed it up
> because it was getting too much. It got too much all day,
> going home, having to get my husband's tea and the kids'
> tea. So I packed it up, then I went cleaning, because it
> was part-time.‡

It was in order to bid down the pay of people like this that
Mrs Thatcher's Government went to the trouble of going to
Geneva to withdraw from an international agreement. Before
it could abolish the Fair Wages Resolution, the British
Government had to revoke Convention 94 of the International
Labour Organisation, a statement of principle which says:
'While producers should be free to compete in matters of
price, design, quality of product and service, it is unfair for
competition to be based on a bidding down of workers'
wages.'

So why does the Government think that it is fair, and in
workers' long-term interest, to have their wages reduced?
Perhaps because this is the first stage in the virtuous circle
of free-market ideology: wage cuts enable British goods and
services to be more competitive in world markets and at the
same time they price other workers into jobs to produce more
of these now competitive products, which will feed back into
higher profits, more investment, higher productivity and, at
last, higher wages again.

---

* *Labour Research*, July 1986.
† Coyle, op. cit., p. 20.
‡ Coyle, op. cit., p. 21.

None of this, however, applies to contracting out public services. Contractors to the public sector are not competing with foreign companies, and contracting out does not create additional employment into which people can 'price themselves'. (There are other flaws with this argument too: contract cleaning is, for instance, one of the more profitable industries – ICC Business Ratios reported in 1983 that the average return on capital in the contract cleaning industry was 27.5 per cent in 1980–1, compared with an average of 10 per cent for British industry as a whole.)

So the only reason why the Government wants to cut the wages of public service workers can be to reduce public spending. And that is not in everybody's interest: it dampens demand, and the demand created by low-paid workers is more productive for the British economy than the demand created by tax cuts for the better-off, more of which are spent on imported manufactured goods. But I do not think that this need be a question of economics; even a monetarist has to ask why the pay of the already very low paid and vulnerable should be reduced simply to obtain a marginal reduction in taxes or Government borrowing – especially at a time when there are so many other items of spending which could be cut, like subsidies to farmers.

So contracting-out can lead to improvements in efficiency, but it is efficiency of the wrong sort – the labour-saving kind rather than the service-improving kind – and it is usually accompanied by unnecessary pay cuts and worse conditions for the workforce (although some councils and health authorities insist on 'fair wages'), and marginally poorer standards. It does not spread wealth; only a small number of people obtain an identifiable benefit: the owners and managers of contractor-companies and their public relations advisers. And any political parties they might support. Brengreen, the parent company of Exclusive, which recruited schoolchildren at £1.72 an hour at Wokingham Hospital, gave £21,480 to the Conservative Party in 1983–4. Conservative MP Michael Forsyth's PR consultancy, Michael Forsyth Associates, is employed by several companies, including Crothalls, part of Pritchards.

And what of the third argument for privatisation: is everyone better off in the long run? No. It is now six years since unemployment first reached three million, and the numbers of long-term unemployed are as high as ever. How long do the unemployed and the low-paid have to wait, watching the growing enrichment of the few, for the benefits to 'trickle down' to them?

Denationalisation

Selling public corporations to the private sector is a policy that developed a momentum of its own. Although dedicated free-marketeers had advocated selling off all publicly owned trading bodies for some time, the 1979 Conservative Government had only promised to return to the private sector the aerospace and shipbuilding industries which the Labour Government had just nationalised, along with the National Freight Corporation. British Aerospace was sold in 1981, and the NFC, now the National Freight Consortium, in 1982. The shipbuilders were in such a poor financial state that their sale was postponed, but a few other anomalous organisations allowed the Government to rehearse its act. Amersham International, part of the UK Atomic Energy Authority, and Britoil, the public-sector North Sea oil company, were also sold off in 1982.

Britoil was the first sell-off to raise a significant amount of money in exchequer terms: over £500 million, the equivalent of a halfpenny off income tax for one year. As a way of reducing the amount the Chancellor needs to borrow to cover the gap between public spending and tax revenue, privatisation had been discovered. The ideology of the free-marketeers, now calling louder than ever for the Post Office, electricity industry, and even schools, to be sold off, followed in the wake of the Conservative Party's desperate need to get away from being the party of higher taxes. When Mrs Thatcher took office, and Geoffrey Howe became Chancellor of the Exchequer, taxes took 38 per cent of Britain's national income. By 1982 that figure had shot up to over 46 per cent. It was at last brought down by Nigel Lawson's pre-election 'tax-cutting' Budget in March 1987 to below 45 per cent.* Had it not been for the substantial revenue from selling British Telecom and British Gas in particular, about £4,000 million and £5,000 million respectively in 1984 and 1986, the tax burden might still be breaking new records.

If you were trying to explain the selling off of public assets to the party of visiting Martians, you might have to go back to basics. John Kay and Mervyn King, in their classic book on how the British Government raises its revenues, *The British Tax System†*, look at the economic fundamentals of privatisation.

> In the Middle Ages, disreputable monarchs would raise revenue by the granting of monopolies. Astute merchants would offer to finance the king's expenditure in return for some exclusive trading rights. No modern government would undertake any procedure so crude; but very similar issues arise, in slightly disguised form, in current proposals for privatisation.

They examine privatisation in relation to the concept of 'economic rent'. Roughly, this means the income that can be derived from the ownership of the right to engage in some profitable activity: to grow crops, drill for oil or, in the Middle Ages, sell monopoly goods such as salt. Many public sector assets were not until recently considered suitable for private ownership, they say, because they represent the economic rent either from 'scarce factors' or from monopolies. 'Much of the revenue of British Airways,' they point out, 'derives from rights to participate in international aviation cartels.' They are

---

* John Hills, *New Statesman*, 13 March 1987.
† Fourth edition, Oxford University Press 1986, p. 186.

particularly scathing about the British Airports Authority, which derives most of its revenue from two sources:

> One is landing charges at Heathrow Airport (a scarce factor). The other is the sale of duty-free goods. Not even medieval kings thought of selling the right to sell goods free of taxes imposed on other traders, and it is more than extraordinary that a modern government should plan to do precisely that.

What are the effects of selling public corporations, compared with the Government's claims for privatisation? The argument for efficiency is harder to prove than in the case of contracting-out. All privatisation candidates were successful and profitable concerns before they were sold off, and in fact the most dramatic improvements in efficiency have taken place in industries which have not yet been privatised. British Steel and British Coal have increased productivity – at the cost of tens of thousands of jobs – whereas British Gas had always been highly profitable and very efficient at extracting and distributing gas. British Telecom has always been very profitable and not so efficient, and there has been no dramatic improvement since privatisation.

As for the short-term effects on the distribution of resources, if the Government were a company, the value of its balance sheet would be reduced, in return for a one-off gain in the profit and loss account. This would not be considered good stewardship of a company's affairs, and were it not for the fact that the company owns a great deal more assets, its directors would risk disqualification. As it is, the shareholders would at least ask awkward questions, and might consider replacing the directors. In the Government's case, however, the 'shareholders' – that is, the citizenry – do not feel as if they own the assets in the first place, and the reduction in the value of their shareholding is neither here nor there. Some of them are merely pleased to enjoy the one-off benefits.

Does denationalisation spread wealth? If receipts from the sale of public assets were applied to the benefit of that section of the population that is poorer than the immediate beneficiaries of the policy, then the policy as a whole would be equitable. But they are not. Capital assets are being sold and the money used to pay for the Government's ordinary running costs. For a Government allegedly motivated by prudence and little else, it is strange to find such a lack of understanding of the difference between 'capital' and 'revenue'.

The distributional consequences of denationalisation are similar to those of selling council houses, only the beneficiaries are concentrated higher up the social scale. The beneficiaries are arranged in a sort of pyramid, at the base of which are the large number of people who benefit a little, and at the top of which are the small number of people who – how shall we put this? – strongly believe in the virtues of free enterprise and the Conservative and Unionist Party.

At the bottom, then, are the large number of taxpayers, who have benefited from the small reduction in income or other taxes, compared with what they would otherwise have been. We do not know how Nigel Lawson would have raised the money had it not been for extra receipts from privatisation, but the burden would probably have fallen on income tax payers, who, with their dependants, make up three-quarters of the adult population. The other quarter, the poorest quarter of the population consisting of pensioners with no significant income other than the State pension and State benefit claimants, did not get anything out of asset sales at all.*

At the next level up are those people who bought shares in privatised companies when they were floated, and who made a profit which they either cashed in immediately or held on to. This profit varied: in the case of British Telecom the first-day profit was 90 per cent, in the case of British Gas it was more like 25 per cent. Although applications were scaled down, the more shares you could afford to bid for the more

---

* Inland Revenue, *Survey of Personal Incomes 1983/84*, HMSO; there were 11.2 million married couples and 9.44 million single people with taxable incomes out of an adult population of about 43 million.

profit you made, so the distribution of profits was heavily skewed towards the better-off.

At the top of the pyramid are 'the professionals': the stags who applied under different names for more shares than they were entitled to, the directors of the privatised companies, and the accountants, lawyers, bankers and underwriters who organised the flotations and earned fees for doing so. The first type of professional is engaged in illegal activity, but the other two types are above board. According to the TUC study 'Privatisation and Top Pay', of December 1985, the average salary rise for the chair/chief executive of newly-privatised companies was 34 per cent within one year of privatisation and 85 per cent within two years – a total rise worth an average of £45,413. The fees paid to City professionals are harder to judge; the sums are enormous – the total fees for British Telecom were £128 million – but we do not know how much profit was made out of them or to what extent they lifted City salaries. Except, that is, for the underwriting fees, £22 million in British Telecom's case, which were 100 per cent profit. The underwriters get paid for agreeing to buy the shares at the issue price if no one else will. Given that the price of British Telecom shares had to err on the cheap side for political reasons, if nothing else, and was five times over-subscribed, the underwriters were hardly taking an audacious risk.

The sale of the Trustee Savings Bank in 1986, though, was a special case. In that instance there was no benefit to the taxpayer because of a spectacular blunder by the Government in selling the TSB at a 100 per cent discount; it gave the TSB away because it failed to realise that it owned it. Although the TSB had been set up and regulated by a series of Acts of Parliament, the Government was under the impression that it was an anomalous form of mutual association which was not owned by anybody. The common-sense interpretation would have been that it was 'owned' by savers past and present and held 'in trust' for them, but neither the narrow confines of the British law nor of the Conservative conception of ownership allowed for this ideal. So the Government permitted the TSB management to float the bank on the stock market, and gave the £800 million-worth of unowned assets that the TSB had accumulated since 1817 to the new company.

However, the narrow legalism of the House of Lords could not cope with the idea of no one owning something, and when rebel TSB depositors approached it with their argument against privatisation, the law lords, in dismissing their case, ruled that 'the State' owned the TSB's assets. In his judgment Lord Templeman said, in a most noble and courteous way, that he thought the Government had bungled it:

> Statutory trustee savings banks and their assets belonged to the State subject to the contractual right of depositors to the return of their deposits and interest. The 1985 Act privatised the statutory trustee savings banks and Parliament decided to present their surplus assets amounting, it was said, to £800 million, to the successor companies. The House [of Lords] was not concerned with the wisdom of that decision.

The result was, according to one commentator, as if the Government were offering to sell you a purse – except that whatever sum you agreed to pay for it, they would put into the purse before handing it over. The TSB received both the proceeds from privatisation (about £1,000 million) and kept the original £800 million, meaning that the shares which were sold for £1,000 million were instantly worth £1,800 million on the day of the flotation – give or take an adjustment for the stock market's assumptions about how much profit it expected the management to earn on its windfall. This guaranteed first-day profit attracted an unprecedented number of share applications with no corresponding benefit to the Treasury. Even the political benefit to the Government's share-ownership crusade was doubtful; far from encouraging the virtues of thrift and responsibility, the flotation gave the impression that stock-market profits are a quick killing made by gulling the credulous.

The beneficiaries of selling off State assets, then, are the better-off, according to the principle of 'the more you've got, the more you get'. The net losers are the vast majority of the population who failed to share in the spoils. Admittedly, ordinary citizens didn't feel that they owned British Telecom and British Gas before they were privatised, and still don't feel that they own British Rail and the Post Office; but they are made even worse off by privatisation because they got no share in something which was rightly theirs. It is as if someone had stolen your savings and, when caught, pointed out that you hadn't touched the money for many years and so wouldn't miss it.

Selling public enterprises to the private sector does not of itself, then, improve efficiency. That can happen just as much while the enterprise is under public ownership. Nor does it spread wealth; on the contrary, it helps to concentrate it. What about the long-term benefit to the economy as a whole? To answer this question we need to consider the ideology of market forces.

Market Forces

All three Conservative claims for privatisation – efficiency, spreading wealth and the benefit to the whole economy – are, as I said at the beginning, interconnected parts of a consistent free-market philosophy. They are based on the doctrine of privateering, in the sense that society is seen as functioning best if individuals are allowed to pursue their own interests, with the role of the law pared down simply to allowing them to do so.

In its extreme form, this applies not just to economic decisions, but to all decisions which can be reduced to money: education, health care, television, planning decisions, immigration. The question that always has to be put to free-marketeers is 'why stop there?' There is no logical reason why the principle should not be extended to political decisions:

better-quality decisions should theoretically be reached if those who cared enough about politics were prepared to pay for the right to vote. Large corporations, who have more at stake, should be allowed to buy as many votes as they think appropriate. Why not abolish local councils and let those who want services contract directly with service-providers? And surely some civil or human rights interfere with the most efficient operation of the free market? What is wrong with slavery voluntarily entered into?

If we are not prepared to witness the return of slavery, the starvation of the poor, old and sick and the spread of disease, then there have to be limits to the operation of the free market. The argument about privatisation is not, therefore, one of whether 'private' is better than 'public', but of where to draw the line between the two.

Mrs Thatcher's Government has exploited the individualism of the age – the cult of privacy and the small, self-contained family unit – to advance the interests of the rich. The shift towards the private sector appears to satisfy people's desire for independence from the State: at the same time it reinforces existing inequalities.

The free-market philosophy is beguiling because it appears to give the individual power. It is pleasant to possess power as a consumer, although it is just as likely that one will be frustrated by the inefficiency and shoddy goods of the private sector. You have no more power over the time of day British Gas engineers will come to deal with problems now it is in the private sector than you did when it was the Gas Board.

The free market fails, however, to give all individuals power equally. Free-market philosophy does not acknowledge that, because people are unequal, merely allowing the free market to take its course – or, worse, encouraging it to take its course – intensifies the divisions in this country between rich and poor, South and North, home-owners and council tenants.

Free-marketeers claim that there is another sort of 'efficiency' which market forces encourage: they do not just raise productivity in private sector enterprise, they improve 'allocative efficiency'. In other words, the free market allocates resources to their most efficient use. But what does that mean? In order to judge the 'efficiency' of local councils versus the private property market in allocating housing, we need to know what we are trying to achieve. If a home 'fit for human habitation' is a basic right of citizens of this country, then the property market alone is not a way of ensuring it, let alone an efficient way, and some means of allocating housing according to need, for example a local council priority points scheme, is needed. In allocating scarce properties to individuals with different wants, the market is more 'efficient' in the economic sense, although its costs are high – it is very expensive to buy, sell and move. But, unless everyone starts with the same amount of money, it doesn't give everyone the same chance.

Most free-marketeers think inequality is a good thing, making everybody richer in the end, so that the poor can be better off and the rich much better off.

It is a strange thing, though, this impartial, all-wise 'free' market. Consider for a moment how it works in practice. A group of men, many of them privately educated, some of them with degrees in Business Administration, meet to discuss the appointment of a new chief executive of Corporate Pile plc. There are two candidates, both men, one privately educated and the other with a degree in Business Administration. (Women, bright young black people who are rising from the shop floor and other unsuitables have been eliminated before the shortlisting stage.) The previous chief executive was paid £80,000, half of which was a performance bonus linked to the share price, before leaving to be director-general of the Pile Industry Association at half the salary but with a guaranteed knighthood.

Both candidates have made it clear they won't pick up the telephone for less than £100,000 a year, which is a matter for the Executive Remuneration Subcommittee, consisting of Corporate Pile's part-time ('non-executive') directors. They have a very high opinion of both candidates and are persuaded by the other directors' arguments that the company's recent growth means that its salary structure should really be compared with Pile Itup International Inc., rather than with its traditional British competitors.

At the Board meeting the privately educated predictably fall out with one another, some of them not thinking the candidate's school to be really first-division, while the MBAs hold ranks and get their man. When he arrives, he proposes an old friend of his as another non-executive director, and proposes to the Executive Remuneration Subcommittee that the full-time directors should have a share option scheme. 'And isn't it about time we reviewed our whole executive reward structure . . . ?'

How much people get paid is as much the result of social and cultural factors as of strictly economic ones. Pay is determined by snobbery, age, office politics, prejudices: most of the time 'the market' is a long distance from most peoples' wages (when was your salary last tested in the labour market?). The main exception to this is in low-paid manual work, especially part-time cleaning, where labour turnover is constant, as an army of workers ceaselessly move from short-term contract to contract looking for better pay and conditions, but where there is a huge reservoir of labour holding pay rates down.

Everybody else has institutional 'rigidities' constructed around their job which help to hold pay up: trade unions, experience, skills, job security, professional qualifications, hierarchical power networks. Of course, Corporate Pile plc would not be paying its new chief executive £100,000 if it could not 'afford' it. But in times of high company profitability (such as the mid-1980s) the division of the spoils is always going to be in favour of those who wield power.

The Conservatives came to power in 1979 pledged 'to restore incentives so that hard work pays'. But how hard do hospital cleaners have to work before it 'pays'? Incentive seems to mean different things to different people, meaning more pay for the rich and less pay for the poor. As Peter Kellner, the *New Statesman*'s political editor, has said:

When Mrs Thatcher uses one of her favourite words,

'incentives', she does not mean incentives to end famine in Africa, or keep old people warm in winter, or help children across busy streets on their way to school. Mrs Thatcher's ideology of 'incentives' has nothing to say about thousands of activities, big and little, that tilt humanity between happiness and misery.*

People-oriented Alternatives to Privatisation

This does not mean that things should be left as they are, or were. One of the spurs to privatisation was the Winter of Discontent at the end of the last Labour Government, when public service workers felt unvalued by the Government and many of the general public did not feel that public sector trade unions were in existence to help them. How, then, can we obtain more efficient, more user-friendly services in a way that isn't biased in favour of the rich?

One way is to improve the morale of public service workers by paying them decent wages and making 'public service' a valued centrepiece of Government policy.

The way public services are organised should be changed so that what is measured is the level and quality of service they provide rather than simply the cost. This is happening in local councils' direct labour organisations in response to privatisation. But privatisation itself is unnecessary and damaging.

Breaking up public services into smaller units – 'decentralis- ation' – could also be a way of making services more respon- sive to the people who are served. In the case of flats, for example, it is more important from the point of view of getting repairs done to give the people living in the same block collective control than it is to sell them their flat.

---

* *New Statesman*, 6 March 1987.

Just as dogmatic privatisation is often irrelevant, however, dogmatic anti-privatisation is equally inappropriate. Economic competition, for example, *can* be a good thing, provided the rules are changed to give everyone a fair chance. Markets should operate, not on the basis of how much money people have to start off with, but as much as possible on the basis of 'one person one vote'.

Left-wingers have always been against monopolies, for instance. One of the traditional responses was to take them into public ownership; this ensured that monopoly power was not abused for the sake of private profit, but it failed to deal fully with the other objection to monopolies, which is that they reduce consumer choice and consumer power.

I am not claiming to know all the answers, but this is the sort of question that should be examined. The solution is not, of course, to sell the monopoly back to the private sector. As it happens, the Government has sold British Telecom and British Gas as intact monopolies to the private sector, but their prices are still 'nationalised', because they are not allowed by law to go up by a percentage below the inflation figure. This has made no difference to consumer choice; what *has* made a difference in the case of British Telecom has been the liberalisation of telecom equipment and the installation of sockets (for which you still have to pay a monopoly £32 price). However, this has in no way benefited those people for whom British Telecom provides a kind of social service, such as people at home who do not make many outgoing telephone calls, and users of public telephones.

What they need is for all households to have, say, vouchers for setting against their standing charge or for buying phonecards – not share perks for those who already have the money for purchasing shares.

If only market forces could be rigged in this way, to balance the permanent bias in favour of the rich. The Conservatives, for example, are very keen to use market forces for forcing down the wages of unskilled manual workers. But what about applying a little competition to the salaries of highly paid professionals? Just occasionally, this happens, with instructive results. After a Labour MP's campaign to end the solicitors' monopoly on the legal work of house-buying was successful, one victim of market forces, a solicitor unable to decipher their wisdom, appeared on a television programme:*

> A bit of competition is quite stimulating, but if you have too much it then becomes a destructive force, and it has driven prices down in this area and perhaps nationally as well by 30 or 40 per cent. Times have become quite stringent financially. I still have three children who go to a fee-paying school and it – to be open about it – it's much more of a struggle to maintain that basis of education.

Note that the 1985 Green Paper did not propose to make it compulsory for local councils to put *professional* services out to tender, although it did mention architectural, legal and quantity surveying services in the context of promoting 'a wider acceptance of the principles of competition across the whole range of local authority activities'.

As Mrs Thatcher said in 1979, 'the things we have in common as a nation far outnumber those that set us apart'. Two of those many things ought to be a legal minimum wage and the right to an equal say as a consumer.

Privatisation is greed masquerading as economics; it is part of what John K. Galbraith calls the present 'revolt of the rich against the poor'.†

---

* 'Scales of Justice', Yorkshire TV, 11 August 1986.
† J. K. Galbraith, *A View from the Stands*, Hamish Hamilton 1987.

Privatisation: A Middle Course

Lord Ezra

Introduction

The argument about public or private ownership has been going on virtually unabated for over forty years, since 1945. It has been primarily a political argument, the confrontation of divergent dogmas; but it has had major economic and social repercussions.

These have arisen from the changes in ownership introduced by successive post-war Labour and Conservative Governments in a significant part of the basic industry of Britain. After the first spate of post-war nationalisation introduced soon after the end of the war in 1945 by the Attlee Government, a degree of denationalisation followed under the succeeding Churchill Government, with further nationalisation during the Wilson Government, leading eventually to the major privatisation policy pursued under the Thatcher regime. The story has not necessarily ended there, as the Labour opposition have stated that, if re-elected, they would bring back into 'social ownership' some of the larger enterprises privatised by the present Conservative Government.

The continued change in the ownership and organisation of large-scale enterprises in the basic sector of industry has undoubtedly been one of the factors leading to lower economic growth in Britain than in other European countries in the post-war period. Worse still, while these enterprises have been under public ownership, successive governments have intervened in their operations for reasons of general policy, thus inhibiting them from conducting their affairs as effectively as might otherwise have been the case.

Although attempts were made, through a series of White Papers which will be described later, to define ground rules for the nationalised industries, they only went part of the way. The sad fact remained that, after forty years, neither the objectives nor the method of operation of the nationalised enterprises were clearly defined; and their most notable feature remained the inconsistency with which governments, of whatever party, approached their affairs.

Thus there is no doubt that a solution still needs to be found. The question is whether the privatisation policy pursued by the present Government will provide such a solution.

In order to answer that question it is necessary to examine, first, the process of nationalisation, and to consider what positive (as well as negative) elements emerged from it; and next to analyse the privatisation measures currently being introduced. Two major issues will require special consideration, namely, the extent to which the privatised enterprises are likely to be subjected to competition, and the position of those enterprises whose monopolistic features are retained on privatisation.

The aim should be to find solutions likely to stand the test of time and unlikely to stimulate governments of differing political views to introduce further structural changes. A number of suggestions will be made with this in mind.

Because of my long involvement in the affairs of the coal industry (from 1947 to 1982), I have drawn on my experience there to illustrate the advantages and disadvantages of nationalised industry during that thirty-five-year period. This analysis is relevant in considering how a more consistent framework can be established in the future.

The Nationalisation Process

The principal period of nationalisation took place under the Attlee Government (1945–51), just as the principal period of denationalisation (or privatisation) took place during the Thatcher Government (1979 onwards). In between these two major periods there was some degree of denationalisation by Conservative Governments and some further degree of nationalisation or renationalisation under Labour Governments.

The motivation of the Attlee Government was to occupy the 'commanding heights' of the economy through public ownership. In practice this meant a large part of transport and energy supply. Outside these key sectors, steel was nationalised (later denationalised and then renationalised) and the Bank of England was also brought into public ownership (this does not seem to have caused any problems then or later).

Public enterprise was not an entirely new concept in 1945. During the inter-war period the London Passenger Transport Board and Imperial Airways were set up to deal with the serious problems arising in London transport and civil aviation. These were attempts to find practical solutions to real problems and did not arouse political controversy.

The nationalisation legislation of the later 1940s was not only larger in scale than anything tried in Britain before but was also clearly politically motivated. Herbert Morrison was the Labour minister who gave most thought to the principles underlying these changes; and he enunciated a formula which has since remained associated with his name. As he saw it, these large enterprises, newly taken over by the State, should be operated independently of it and in the public interest. Their revenues should 'not be less than sufficient for meeting all their outgoings properly chargeable to revenue account . . . on an average of good and bad years.'* In other words, they

---

* The quotation is from the Coal Industry Nationalisation Act 1946, Clause 1(4)(c). Similar words were introduced in the other Nationalisation Acts.

should both serve the public interest *and* achieve commercial viability.

This was a fine concept in principle, as applied to largely monopolistic enterprises providing the nation with basic products or services. The trouble was that the application of the concept was not worked out in any detail. The Acts nationalising the various basic industries were very largely concerned with the process of taking over the assets and relatively little with the conduct of the business in its new public form. The Coal Industry Act of 1946 was typical of the cursory way in which the matter was dealt with. The newly appointed National Coal Board was charged with the duty of 'making supplies of coal available, of such qualities and sizes, in such quantities and at such prices as seem to them best calculated to further the public interest in all respects' (Clause 1(1)(c). Apart from the need to break even over a period of good and bad years, as mentioned above, little more was stated about how the enterprise should be managed.

Right from the start, the underlying Morrisonian principle was breached. In spite of the explicit intention of leaving it to the management themselves to fix the prices for their products, having regard to the public interest, the Government persuaded the Coal Board to continue the 'gentlemen's agreement' reached with the former coal owners during the war to peg prices at their 1939 level. Thus coal prices in Britain were kept well below the world market level throughout the period of the Attlee Government, and indeed until 1957 when the market situation fundamentally changed through the influx of large quantities of oil from the Middle East.

During the first ten years of nationalisation, although coal was in short supply, limited quantities, by agreement with Government, were made available for export. The world market price was charged for this, and was up to £2 a ton higher than the pegged home price. In the period between 1946 and 1956 some 2 billion tons of coal were produced and used in the UK. Had normal pricing applied, the NCB could have built up a substantial reserve fund which would have helped to see it through the ensuing decade when oil substantially underpriced coal.

To make matters worse, when American coal at higher cost had to be imported during the period of coal shortage to help out in the power stations, the Government decided that the NCB should pay the difference. This was an example of the Government imposing a social obligation on the coal industry much to the detriment of its commercial wellbeing.

Prices remained an issue on which Government regularly intervened in the affairs of the nationalised industries; but while, during the early post-war period, the pressure was to keep prices down, in later years, particularly under the present Government, the Treasury sought to keep prices up. Their pressure was quite overt; indeed, in 1985, the gas, electricity and water industries were forced to increase their prices above what the enterprises regarded as a desirable commercial level, and this was generally seen as a means of raising additional indirect taxes.

Capital investment was another area in which Governments regularly intervened. While it was laid down in the Nationalisation Acts that, in matters of substantial capital outlay, the Boards should 'act on lines settled from time to time with the approval of the Minister', it was clearly not envisaged that the amount of investment should be determined by external political factors. And yet this is what happened. In the early post-war years the nationalised industries were regarded as a convenient means of reviving the economy and the pressure from Government was to maximise investment. This was succeeded by the period of 'fine tuning' and the Government 'tried to regulate the pace of the whole economy by year-to-year adjustments in national-ised industries' capital spending'.* Still later it became Government policy to restrict expenditure by the nationalised industries on the ground that it was 'crowding out' private expenditure, which was favoured by the Conservative Government of the day.

---

* 'Lessons of Public Enterprise', ed. Michael Shanks, Jonathan Cape (1963), p. 22.

Intervention in wage negotiations also developed over the years. It was laid down in the Coal Industry Nationalisation Act, that the Board should establish joint machinery for 'the settlement by negotiation of terms and conditions of employment, with provision for reference to arbitration in default of such settlement'.* In the early years of nationalisation the system worked reasonably well and arbitration proved an effective means of settling disagreements on wages and conditions. But in due course the unions became restive about arbitration, alleging, rightly or wrongly, that the arbitrators were being unduly influenced by pressure from Government. In subsequent years, although the appearance of negotiations between employers and employees in the various nationalised industries was maintained, Government increasingly intervened, mainly informally but sometimes quite openly.

An ambivalent position was often adopted towards closures in those industries where this was relevant, namely coal and the railways. This was especially the case with Conservative Governments who, while publicly favouring closures in general on economic grounds, were often privately hesitant about particular closures which could create problems in specific areas. This was another element of confusion in Government's dealings with nationalised industries.

The unsatisfactory relationship between Government and nationalised industries was noted quite soon after nationalisation and led to growing public pressure to improve the situation; and in turn led to a series of White Papers (in 1961, 1967 and 1978) which attempted to provide a clearer framework. This only succeeded to some degree. Indeed, in particular instances further elements of confusion were introduced. For example, under the statutes the industries were required to break even over a period of good and bad years, but the 1961 White Paper introduced the concept of annual financial targets. Which concept was to take precedence? In the 1967 White Paper it was laid down that prices should reflect long-

*Coal Industry Nationalisation Act 1946, Clause 46(1)(a).

run marginal costs. But this introduced an element of ambiguity because of the subjective thinking that was involved in making long-run cost estimates. In any event, Governments very soon resumed their intervention on pricing for short-run reasons.

In the 1978 White Paper the concept of 'external financing limits' (EFLs) was introduced. This began to take pride of place among the financial controls imposed by Government on the nationalised industries. Unfortunately, it was a concept which lent itself to a large degree of manipulation. While it was undoubtedly a useful discipline for those enterprises in financial difficulty – the equivalent of the bank manager who imposes a limit on the overdraft facilities available to a customer whose credit became overstretched – it was used for other purposes in the case of those public enterprises generating cash, such as gas and electricity. Here the concept of the 'negative EFL' was introduced so that the Government could siphon off the surplus cash rather than leaving it in the hands of the enterprise in accordance with normal commercial practice.

Thus it can be concluded that, in spite of the attempt made in the White Papers to clarify relations between government and the nationalised industries, little was achieved and indeed some new anomalies were introduced. However, it should not also be concluded that because of the weakness in Government/enterprise relationships, all had been going wrong with the enterprises in the forty years of nationalised industry. On the contrary, there have been some notable achievements which are worth recalling.

Perhaps surprisingly in the light of later events, industrial relations were much improved in the period immediately following nationalisation. In the case of the coal industry this situation lasted effectively until about 1969. It was noticeable that during the period of massive pit closures in the 1960s, brought about through the competitive pressure of oil, the operation was carried out reasonably harmoniously between unions and management. The worsening of relations at the end of the 1960s coincided with the mounting crisis between

Government and unions generally. It was in 1969 that Barbara Castle's *In Place of Strife* was abandoned; the restiveness of the unions in the nationalised industries at this period was the reflection of a wider malaise. On a more positive side, the consultative procedures established under the Nationalisation Acts were a major step forward in the involvement of unions and employees in the enterprise, and in normal circumstances paid off well. Naturally, from time to time, either because of personalities or for extraneous reasons, the potential for satisfactory industrial relations existing within the framework of the nationalised industries could be overridden.

This leads to the question of motivation. It is often held that this is bound to be weak in a nationalised industry. I did not find this to be so – at any rate in the coal industry. In management, the motivation of the mining engineer and the other professional personnel was very high. The challenge of the job to be done, and of the natural obstacles to be overcome, transcended the question of ownership, to which so much attention has been attached in more recent times. Equally, the principal motivation that I discerned among the miners was loyalty to the pit. This must be similar to the sailor's attachment to his ship. It was strongly felt and at times emotive. It seemed to me that these two elements of motivation were as important as anything in the private sector and needed to be suitably harnessed.

I believe progress was also made in the field of consumer relations. The Nationalisation Act decreed that consumers' councils should be set up. These varied according to the industry. In the case of coal there were two – the Industrial Coal Consumers Council and the Domestic Coal Consumers. There is still a long way to go in ensuring that consumers' interests are effectively safeguarded vis-à-vis large-scale enterprise. Nonetheless, I consider that an important step forward was made in the setting up and operation of consumers' councils in the nationalised industries.

Another area in which success was achieved was that of purchasing. The nationalised industries buy substantial quantities of equipment and services to run their business. They thus have a considerable potential impact on the rest of industry. The policy consistently pursued by the nationalised industries has stimulated British-based suppliers to meet their requirements on a competitive basis. For example, when I left the NCB in 1982 they were purchasing 96% of their requirements in this country and their total annual buying expenditure amounted to over £1 billion. Similar results were achieved in the other major nationalised industries.

The purchase of so much on a competitive basis from home sources was made possible by a close partnership between purchaser and supplier in research and development, innovation and quality control. But at the end of the day the goods were only purchased if they were of the required standard and at competitive prices. In this way over £10 billion of UK purchases were generated by the nationalised sector.

A significant spin-off was the amount of export business achieved in consequence of competitively supplying the large-scale basic enterprises in the UK. For example, in mining machinery, UK firms penetrated into most of the world's markets and in the early 1980s were exporting to the tune of £200 to £300 million annually.

The mutually beneficial interrelationship of the public and private sectors of industry, as it developed over the years, was one of the most positive features of nationalisation. It tended on the whole not to be interfered with by Government and was developed in different ways in the different sectors. A number of joint enterprises were established which operated on commercial lines and were generally profitable for the partners. In the case of coal, these covered such areas as mining consultancy, fuel distribution, heat service and chemical by-products. The NCB also actively assisted the mining machinery manufacturers in their export operations by supplementing their technical expertise and demonstrating the use of their plant.

In considering the future regime for the nationalised industries, and in particular whether and to what extent privatisation is the answer, it is necessary to analyse experience in nationalisation so far. This has been the purpose of the foregoing paragraphs. What emerges is that the principal weakness has lain in relations with Government. Whether the original Morrisonian concept was a valid proposition or not, no one can tell. It was never given a chance. Government intervened from the start and has not stopped intervening in the affairs of the nationalised industries. This has been the case particularly in regard to prices, investment, wages and closures (where they arose).

On the other hand, there were many positive features, especially where the industries were allowed to get on with the job. There were improved methods of consultation with employees, which had a beneficial effect in the early years; consumers' interests were better safeguarded than previously; motivation and interest in the job and place of work were stimulated; and a positively orientated purchasing policy helped to spread competitiveness in important parts of the private sector, especially in machinery and equipment.

Perhaps their most important contribution was that they enabled basic sectors of the economy to be reorganised in a positive manner after a period of great difficulty. This was especially true of the coal industry, which not only inevitably suffered from lack of investment during the war but had been through a traumatic period of dissension and internecine competition in the inter-war period. This was replaced by a single, comprehensive structure and coordinated investment, marketing and research policies. Without those policies at that time, the industry could not have provided sorely needed supplies. And when the difficult times came, it was easier to cope with the problems on a coordinated basis than on the fragmented inter-war basis which led inevitably to Government intervention.

In looking to the future organisation of these enterprises, the challenge will be to overcome the elements of weakness while retaining the elements of strength. To what extent has privatisation provided the answer? This will be examined in the succeeding section.

The Privatisation Process

The present Government's initial approach to privatisation was set out in the Conservative Manifesto of 1979. Criticising Labour's plans to extend nationalisation, it indicated the intention to sell back the recently nationalised aerospace and shipbuilding industries and to encourage private investment in the National Freight Corporation and in the bus services.

It also stated that the Conservative Party wished to see 'those industries that remain nationalised running more successfully and we will therefore interfere less with their management'. In fact, as has been shown in the previous section, the present Government have interfered as much as previous Governments and have implicitly admitted this in the course of public speeches and debates introducing various privatisation measures.

The Government's rationale for privatisation was set out at some length in a major speech by Mr John Moore, as Financial Secretary at the Treasury, on 1 November 1983. By then a certain amount of progress had been made in the plans for privatisation and Mr Moore's object was to explain the Government's reasoning more fully because it was 'poorly understood'.

He began by emphasising the importance of the nationalised industries in the economy. They represented about 10 per cent of the GDP and some 13 per cent of total investment, employing about 1½ million people 'many of whom are extremely able'. He then went on to demonstrate that the original Morrisonian concept could not work. Enterprises in the public sector could not be left to their own devices by Government. They had to abide by public-sector rules, involving constraint on borrowing, investment and a host of other matters. This was bound to lead to confusion in the minds of management as to whether they were to operate commercially or as a public service.

He referred to the attempts to define more clearly the

financial objectives of the nationalised industries in the White Papers of 1961, 1967 and 1978. He did not think these had been particularly successful. Possibly the most effective control was that affecting cash by means of the external financing limits, 'but even this system is subject to severe strain'.

He considered that the purpose of these various changes was 'to compensate for the lack of market forces by imposing surrogate market forces on the industries'. Governments, he wrote, had systematically set about creating external stimuli which tried to provide pressures similar to that provided by market mechanisms. He considered that, under the Government's policy of privatisation, competition would replace the surrogate market with the real market and that the 'control philosophy' which had evolved over the years would be brought to its logical conclusion.

The Government claim there are many advantages in privatisation, notably that 'managers are set free to manage and new opportunities are opened up'. The evidence for these advantages is stated to arise from the improved results since privatisation of such companies as Cable & Wireless, Associated British Ports, Amersham and National Freight. But these enterprises were already doing reasonably well before, or had a clear prospect for improvement, otherwise they could not have been sold off to the private sector. It is a necessary feature of these transactions that the assets being put on the market are saleable and show good prospects. It is therefore open to some debate whether and to what extent the improvements which have taken place since privatisation would have occurred anyway. Nevertheless, it is true that under a private regime managements can operate more freely and respond more quickly to external events and market opportunities.

It is also argued that there are benefits to employers, especially through share ownership. It is held that this motivates them, and the National Freight Corporation is cited as an example. In fact, it is an exception. The company was bought out by the management and the work force, and they have achieved success. But in the case of other privatisations the shares were sold to the public at large, with the employees taking up a relatively small proportion. Although share ownership can help to motivate, other factors are at least as important, if not more so. One of these is effective participation in the affairs of the enterprise. For this type of motivation the enterprise does not need to be in the private sector. During the 1970s some very effective forms of participation were developed in the nationalised industries which, in this regard, were ahead of many firms in the private sector. Another form of motivation, particularly important at times of high unemployment, is a sense of security of tenure. Basically this depends on the sector in which the business is located; whether it is public or private has less relevance. Over the years, employees, rightly or wrongly, have regarded nationalised industries as providing greater job security than the private sector.

It is contended that great benefits accrue to the consumer as a result of privatisation, with the increase of competition. But here again competition is not necessarily confined to the private sector. For example, the railways, although nationalised, have had for years to contend with the competition of road and air transport. On the other hand, as will be discussed later, the transference of monopolies from the public to the private sector does not, of itself, increase competition. In other words, competition is not relevant to the type of ownership of a business but to the nature of its activity and its relative strength, whether public or private, in the market place. There has been a tendency for the Government and their supporters to exaggerate the beneficial effects of privatisation simply to justify its extension.

Generally speaking, nationalised industries have been at the larger end of business enterprises. This has raised the question of the form in which they should be sold off. In some cases the enterprises were in a natural competitive position, such as Associated British Ports, which was in competition with other ports around the country, or National Freight, which was in competition with other carriers. Elsewhere it was possible to separate the enterprise to be sold from its parent without too much difficulty. Examples of this are Amersham International and Jaguar. Amersham was previously called the Radiochemical Centre Ltd. and was part of the UK Atomic Energy Authority. The shares in the renamed Amersham company were sold to the public in February 1982 and heavily over-subscribed (which raised the question of whether the Government were, in their desire to sell public assets, pitching the price too low).

Jaguar was part of BL, producing cars at the quality end of the range. Along with the other parts of BL, it had suffered badly in the 1970s but began to recover in the early 1980s. It was privatised in August 1984 and has since done well.

There have been instances which have not been so clear-cut. British Aerospace, which was established as a public corporation in 1977 under the previous Labour administration, was one of the first targets for privatisation announced by the Conservative Party, and legislation to this end was put in hand very soon after the general election of 1979. The Government gave some thought to dividing the aircraft and dynamics business and floating them off separately, but eventually, after lengthy consultations with the management and financial advisers, decided against this. The reasoning was that such a division would weaken the company's international competitiveness, which was a key objective in the privatisation process.

In presenting the measure to the House of Commons at the Second Reading debate on 20 November 1979, Sir Keith Joseph (then Secretary of State for Industry) recognised that the British Aerospace organisation was 'a very successful and important national asset'. The reason for privatising it did not appear to be that it had failed as a public enterprise but that it could be 'even more successful and effective as a private company'. It may well be that, as a private enterprise, the management could operate more speedily and with greater flexibility; nevertheless, the continuing involvement of Government in its affairs is unavoidable. For one thing, there are the substantial defence contracts for which the Government is the sole customer. For another, major overseas contracts very often require 'soft' loans from Government to compete with tenders from other countries where Government support is quite overt. This illustrates the blurred line which exists between public and private enterprises in certain sectors, particularly where Government is a major contractor.

The privatisation of the National Bus Company illustrates a situation in which the Government decided to sell off the assets piecemeal. While it would have been possible to dispose of the enterprise as a whole, the Government no doubt concluded that it would be more in keeping with the deregulation of coach traffic (introduced in the Transport Act of 1986) to split the disposal of the enterprise into no less than seventy operating companies before selling it off. This, however, has led to complications. There was a slow start in interesting any buyers. Disposals have since speeded up; but in all cases sales have been to the existing management. The extent to which this will introduce effective competition remains to be seen. This piecemeal disposal also raises the issue of the Victoria Coach Station, currently owned and operated by the National Bus Company. To whom will it be sold when the operating companies have been disposed of, and how will it be managed? It is already causing severe problems of congestion in the Victoria area and is being used far in excess of its planned capacity.

The British Technology Group, set up in 1981, is the successor to the National Enterprise Board (NEB) formed by the previous Labour Government. Its aim, under Labour, was to invest in a wide range of enterprises in the private sector to introduce a public involvement and to stimulate expansion. This concept was contrary to the philosophy of the Conservative Government which limited its role to facilitating the transfer of technology from the universities to commercial enterprises and charged it with the divestment of all its company shares. A large number of these investments have been sold off by individual negotiation. One of the most important has been INMOS, which was formed by the NEB in 1976 to design and manufacture integrated circuits or 'silicon chips' in competition with Japanese and American firms. It was sold to Thorn EMI for £95 million in July 1984. Thorn itself, however, got into some difficulty thereafter, and some doubts were expressed in the media as to whether this was a suitable acquisition on their part.

Britoil and Enterprise Oil were respectively formed by hiving off parts of the British National Oil Corporation (since abolished) and British Gas (since privatised). Both share issues were under-subscribed and the companies subsequently ran into difficulties along with the rest of the oil sector as a result of the weakening of the oil price. These were instances when initial shareholders, including employees, will have seen the value of their shares diminish, although in the longer term they may recover if the oil price returns nearer to previous levels.

A curious form of privatisation was that relating to the Trustee Savings Bank. There was some legal doubt about its ownership. The Government decided that it was owned by the TSB Group itself, even though for many years it had acted as an arm of Central Government through its involvement with the national savings movement. The flotation was delayed by battles in the courts, particularly in Scotland where it was claimed that the Scottish TSB was a separate entity and should not be sold off with the rest. Eventually, the flotation for the whole enterprise went ahead. The shares were heavily over-subscribed and ended up at a premium. This is not surprising as the proceeds of the flotation went back into the Group, thus substantially increasing their assets.

It could be contended that the privatisation measures introduced up to the end of 1986, excluding British Telecom and British Gas (which will be dealt with later), were all in competitive sectors of the economy, and that selling off these enterprises, and removing them from the protective link with government, increased the competitive pressures to which they were subject. This, according to Conservative philosophy, would make them more efficient. But it can be seen from the foregoing paragraphs that there were considerable differences and impacts in the various privatisation measures.

In some instances the enterprises were already efficient and could have been expected to continue so. In other cases (Aerospace being the main example) the Government connection was an integral part of the business and was bound to continue. In yet others (such as TSB) the enterprise was not owned by the Government at all.

One clear benefit to the Government from all these measures (except TSB), was the money they obtained either directly as accruals to the Treasury or indirectly by reducing the financial burden of those parts of the business still remaining in public hands.

However, even if the arguments in favour of privatisation were not as simple and straightforward as the Government contended, there was, on the whole, no particular reason (with the possible exception of Aerospace) why they should have remained in public hands; and the greater freedom of action and flexibility provided by privatisation have been advantageous. It is therefore to be hoped that succeeding governments, with different political views, would not consider it necessary or desirable to bring them back into the public sector, with the dislocation and discontinuity which this would entail.

Quite different considerations arise in the privatisation of natural monopolies, such as British Telecom, British Gas and other possible candidates. These will now be examined.

Privatising the Monopolies

It is generally agreed that there have been two phases in the Government's privatisation programme. The first phase covered enterprises which were already in a competitive situation. It could be held, as indicated previously, that transferring the ownership to the private sector would underline and further stimulate that competitive situation.

The second phase, which started with British Telecom and British Gas, covered natural monopolies which were transferred as such into the private sector. Other enterprises for which the Government has prepared privatisation proposals include British Airways, the British Airports Authority and the regional water authorities. The intention appears to be to privatise all these in their present form.

In considering the privatisation of monopolies, it is relevant to recall what is stated in the Conservative Party's 1983 Manifesto. This said that 'merely to replace state monopolies by private ones would be to waste an historic opportunity. So we will take steps to ensure that these new firms do not exploit their powerful positions to the detriment of consumers or their competitors.' This issue was referred to by Mr John Moore in his speech of 1 November 1983, to which reference has already been made. In that he said, 'we are not so naive as to think that an unrestrained monopoly in the private sector would be less inclined to exploit its position than the monopolies in the public sector'. He then went on to describe how this would be avoided by regulation and other means. In a later speech given on 17 July 1985, he dealt with the subject in more depth, saying that privatisation had proved 'of such major benefit over the last five years' that it had been decided to extend it progressively to the so-called natural monopolies. He concluded that 'regulated private ownership of natural monopolies is preferable to nationalisation', and added that 'those who criticise the decision to privatise utilities as being a Treasury-inspired fund-raising exercise have just not considered the facts'.

The view expressed by Mr Moore that private monopolies were better than public monopolies was described in a special article in The Economist* as being 'plausible but disingenuous'. A number of other commentators also expressed concern. For example, the Scotsman† considered that the

---

* 21 December 1985.
† 13 March 1984.

privatisation process was in danger of creating new monopolies in place of old, and that the Government was being
exclusively concerned with the question of ownership,
whereas in fact it should have been concerned with market
organisation, liberalisation and greater competitiveness.

This is a theme which has been taken up in greater depth in
two important publications, *Privatisation and the Natural
Monopolies*,* and *Privatisation and Regulation*.† These two
publications represent the main sources so far in what will
undoubtedly become a continuing subject of major debate.

The regulation of private monopolies is a new experience
in the United Kingdom, although it has long been in evidence
in the United States, where a very comprehensive form of
regulation of public utilities is considered normal practice.
However, in spite of the American example, the regulatory
bodies set up in the United Kingdom in connection with
British Telecom and British Gas have deliberately been
established with much broader terms of reference than their
American counterparts. Serious concern was expressed about
this during debates in Parliament. It was felt that the
regulatory bodies would neither have the powers nor the
personnel effectively to control the vast organisations for
which they were made responsible. Furthermore, the terms of
the licence in the case of British Telecom and of the regulations
in the case of British Gas were also widely drawn. These
aspects will be dealt with in the succeeding paragraphs which
relate specifically to the natural monopolies so far privatised.
Subsequently, consideration will be given to the further
monopolies in the pipeline.

British Telecom   The first step in the privatisation of British
Telecom (BT) was the British Telecommunications Act of
1981 which set it up as a public corporation separate from the
Post Office. The 1981 Act also introduced some measure of
competition or liberalisation, particularly in the supply and

---

* Public Policy Centre in London, 1985.
† Clarendon Press, 1986.

sale of terminal equipment. There followed the Tele-communications Act of 1984 in which BT was privatised through the process of selling off rather more than half the company to the public.

The method of selling the shares in BT is important because it was the procedure followed in the case of British Gas and will presumably also be applied in the cases of other monopolies to be privatised. The Government's stated intention in selling these shares in previously publicly owned enterprises is not only to privatise them but also to spread the shareholding as widely as possible. In order to achieve this, the shares were offered on favourable terms, with the result that they were traded at a substantial premium when placed on the market. This process, as complemented later by the British Gas issue, has begun to give the impression that shareholders are bound to gain from acquiring shares on privatisation and that no risks attach to them. This could well create problems with more speculative issues, such as that of British Airways, recently placed on the market.

The major criticism made of the privatisation of BT is that the liberalising process was not taken far enough, with the consequence that it has remained a virtual monopoly under privatisation. Only two specific measures of competitiveness were introduced into the system. The first was the liberalisation in the supply and sale of terminal equipment. The second was the grant of a limited licence to Mercury to run a telecommunications network. This licence runs until 1990 and is restricted to 3 per cent of the network. No other licences will be granted in that period. Apart from these two qualifications, BT remains in monopolistic control of the telecommunications services in the UK. It was for this reason that the regulatory body, Oftel, was established. Time will tell whether it will be sufficiently strong to cope with the very large organisation for which it has been made responsible.

Another cause for concern relates to pricing. Professor Littlechild, who was entrusted with the task of proposing how BT's profitability could be regulated in view of its monopolistic situation, proposed the formula for limited price rises which was subsequently adopted in the licence. This was the famous X minus 3 formula, meaning that the price could not be increased in any one year more than 3 percentage points below the rate of inflation. This seemed at the time to be a reasonable formula until it was realised that the formula applied to the generality of BT's charges, and not to individual markets. The result is that they are at liberty to charge more for particular services and less for others. This indeed is what happened in 1986, with domestic charges being increased more than the formula, and business charges less, presumably because of the competitiveness of Mercury in the latter sector.

British Gas   In the run-up to the privatisation of British Gas, which occurred in 1986, there was much debate about the form in which this should take place. A first step in liberalising the market for gas was taken in the Oil and Gas (Enterprises) Act 1982. This removed the statutory monopoly of British Gas to supply their own gas through the network which they operated and to leave it open to private enterprise to lease the use of the network for the transmission of their own gas to their customers. So far as is known, no use has been made of this facility, presumably because suitable terms could not be agreed for leasing the pipelines. No further measures of liberalisation have been introduced, although a number of options were available. For example, it would have been possible to leave the national and regional networks in the hands of British Gas while enabling producers of gas from the North Sea or elsewhere to have access to this network on freely negotiable terms. It would also have been possible to separate off the regional networks and the regional supply of gas. However, none of these options were adopted and the decision was reached to privatise British Gas as a whole. It was unclear during debates in Parliament how this would necessarily change – for better or worse – the service currently offered by British Gas.

In the case of British Gas, as in that of BT, a regulatory body was set up and a similar debate took place in Parliament as to the powers and personnel which should be attributed to this body. The Government resisted all attempts to extend these powers or to strengthen the regulatory body. The pricing formula devised for British Gas was different from that for BT in that it was accepted that prices in the industrial market for gas were subject to competition from other fuels. In the case of the domestic market, which was dominated as to 60 per cent by gas, it was felt that a price formula was necessary. The formula that was eventually agreed allowed for the consumer to get some benefit from the increased operating efficiency of the corporation but left the corporation free to add into the price any extra costs arising from its purchase of gas in the North Sea or elsewhere. In addition, there was some vagueness about the standing charge. It therefore seemed that in the case of gas, as well as that of BT, the attempt to find a formula to restrain predatory pricing could run into difficulties.

British Airways   The privatisation of British Airways raises different issues. There is an international regulatory framework for all airlines operating services from one country to another. The impact of this system could not be affected by privatising British Airways. However, domestic airlines could be deregulated and route transfers made between UK airlines in their international traffic. In fact, some route transfers took place in 1984 when British Airways and British Caledonian swapped their Saudi Arabian and South American routes. In the 'Pathfinder' prospectus issued on 8 January 1987 relating to the privatisation of British Airways, the Government gave a commitment that there would be no further route transfers between British airlines. This was clearly to remove uncertainties. The Government also stated that British Airways would be 'treated no differently from any other British airline'.

The difficulty about British Airways as a private investment is that it is subject to international factors quite outside its control, even though much has been achieved by greater efficiency. For example, when the value of sterling increased in 1981 and 1982, the operating profit of British Airways was much reduced. Subsequently, with the decline in sterling, profits increased, and these were further helped by the fall in the price of oil. However, the reduction in the American tourist trade, as a result of Chernobyl and Libyan terrorism, means that there is likely to be a noticeable reduction in British Airways' pre-tax profit for the year to 31 March 1987. It is no doubt for this reason that the flotation was aimed more at institutional investors than at the small shareholder whom the Government were keen to encourage with the flotations of British Telecom and British Gas.

British Airports In listing the proposed measures for privatisation in their 1983 Manifesto, the Conservative Party stated that 'as many as possible of Britain's airports shall become private sector companies'. In practice, this has come down to the proposed privatisation of the British Airports Authority. The debate about this has centred on whether BAA's London airports (Heathrow/Gatwick/Stansted) should be kept together on privatisation or separated. BAA have argued strongly that the present unity of the organisation should be maintained, since it has performed successfully over the years.

The argument for maintaining it as a single organisation is therefore strong. However, the argument for selling it off to private investors raises questions. The first is what benefit would be achieved? The BAA derive their revenue from two sources: aircraft landing and handling fees, and from a range of commercial services to passengers which are franchised to private enterprises on a competitive basis. These functions would continue under privatisation. No doubt it could be argued that in the private sector the BAA would have greater flexibility and could turn to other sources than Government for financing their various developments. But there is a second question. As they would effectively retain a monopoly of London's airports, who would ensure that they operated this monopoly properly?

BAA already largely operate through third parties who are in the private sector. How strong is the case for also putting them in the private sector? And if so, is there a need for a regulatory body to supervise BAA's operations? Such a body could apply a similar principle to that which pertained to growth in prices by British Gas and BT, namely, an X-Y formula. This would limit the rate of increase in charges at British airports and prevent a possible abuse of monopoly.

Water The Government's plans to privatise the water industry were set out in a White Paper issued in February 1986.* It was expected that a Bill would be introduced into Parliament in the following November. Privatisation of water, however, raises particularly complex issues, and it was not surprising that the Government announced a postponement, with the object, no doubt, of letting other less complex privatisation measures go through.

The existing ten Water Authorities (nine in England and one in Wales) were set up under the Water Act 1973. The principle was that a single body in each region should plan and control all uses of water in each river catchment. The responsibilities of the single authority included water supply, sewerage and sewage disposal, as well as water resource planning, pollution control, fisheries, flood protection, navigation, water recreation and environmental conservation. There were one or more river basins in each authority and they were responsible for all the functions specified above.

There seems to be general agreement that the principle of integrated river basin management as operated under the 1973 Act has been successful and indeed has attracted a great deal of attention from other countries. For this reason, the Government decided to privatise the water industry under its present organisation and with its present responsibilities. But this immediately raised two problems. The first was that the privatised regional water bodies would be complete natural monopolies in their respective areas. The second was that a large part of their current activities as public bodies are concerned with regulation. How were these two problems to be dealt with?

---

* Issued as Cmnd. 9734.

The Government's answer was to propose the appointment of a Director-General of Water Services who would effectively regulate the water regulators. With the exception of flood protection and land drainage, which would be handed over to specially created public bodies, the privatised regional Water Authorities would continue to exercise all the regulatory functions that they already perform. But many of these functions, while totally acceptable in a public body, would become questionable in a privately owned enterprise. For example, the Authorities have the duty of tackling river pollution by controlling both their own discharges and those of others. But once they were privatised it could be contended, rightly or wrongly, that they were capable of exercising this power discriminately in their favour so as to achieve a commercial benefit from it. While this is the sort of matter which could be referred to the Director-General, the basic doubts would still remain.

In a debate on the subject in the House of Lords on 21 May 1986, speakers from all parties were concerned about the problem of reconciling so much public duty with privatisation. The conclusion reached by many was that privatisation of the water industry, as it now stands, would not be an acceptable arrangement. A clearer distinction would be necessary between the regulatory functions of the existing Water Authorities and their commercial activities. Whereas it could be contended that the latter activities might be privatised, even though they would remain a monopoly, the hiving off to a specially constituted public authority of the regulatory functions seemed highly desirable. But if this were done, the whole principle of integrated river base management would be jeopardised. This dilemma over the privatisation of the Water Authorities is an illustration of the difficulty that can be caused by putting into the private sector public enterprises in their existing form and without major modification.

Conclusions

It has been shown that the Government's privatisation programme can be divided into two parts. Firstly, there was privatisation of the whole or parts of public enterprises which were already in a competitive situation. The logic of privatisation varied in each case but, generally speaking, it can be argued that this part of the public sector could on balance do better within the competitive pressures of the private sector.

The second situation, relating to privatisation of the so-called natural monopolies, is altogether different. There are, in fact, two ways of dealing with this situation. One is to privatise the enterprise as it stands. This has the merit of simplicity, retains the existing management and generally has their support, and offers to shareholders a substantial degree of security in the value of their shares. It is the route which has so far been taken by the Government.

The other approach is to introduce a measure of competition before privatisation. This has only been followed to a limited degree; but it has been contended in Parliament, in the press and elsewhere that much further thought should have been given to this approach. The risks of a privatised monopoly abusing its position are considerable, in spite of the regulatory bodies set up. The Government themselves have spoken of the possibility of 'regulatory capture'. This occurs when the regulatory body becomes captive to the enterprise it is meant to be regulating. Such instances have arisen in the United States.

There are a number of options which could have been examined to establish a greater degree of competition in connection with the natural monopolies. At a conference organised by the *Financial Times* in November 1983, dealing with the economy and privatisation, I drew attention to the fact that there are certain public enterprises which, as an essential part of their activities, provide a national 'network'. In this category could be included British Telecom who operate the television and cable links, the gas and electricity enterprises who operate the distribution mains for their fuels, the water boards who operate the water distribution system, and the railways who operate the rail lines. Based on this concept, I suggested that the networks, because of the obvious need to avoid unnecessary and uneconomic duplication, could be retained in public hands but that their use could be licensed to private operators on a competitive basis. This approach has only been adopted to a limited degree. In the case of British Telecom, Mercury has been licensed to use the network up to a limit of 3 per cent until 1990, when the situation will be reviewed. In the case of gas and electricity, legislation has been introduced to enable other producers to use their networks under licence, but the difficulty of agreeing suitable terms has so far inhibited progress. Much could have been gained by examining these options more fully in the case of the privatisation of British Telecom and British Gas. This would, however, have led to a delay in the privatisation measures and therefore a delay in the Government receipt of the substantial sums realised by the sale of shares.

Apart from the network approach, there is the franchising approach. This could apply particularly to the Water Authorities. In a number of countries abroad, notably France, a distinction is drawn between the public responsibility for water supply and the commercial aspects of handling the supply and of providing the capital for the associated works. On this basis, the existing regional water supply organisations in the UK would retain their public functions but would be required to franchise the operation of the water supply itself. Under franchise arrangements, the Water Authority could lay down the regulations which would have to be observed as well as terms of the arrangement and the period during which it would last. The opportunity to provide the services would be put out to public tender.

As a variant of this, there could be an extension of operational contracts. These would be contracts for the provision of the services needed for the supply of water, plus some provision for meeting capital cost. Again, these contracts would be put out to tender and therefore a competitive element would be introduced. As water is a natural monopoly, it is difficult to see how competition can be introduced in the supply of water itself, since to provide the consumer with a choice of water suppliers would be a wasteful system. On the other hand, it should be quite possible to segregate off various parts of the water supply process and put those out to competition.

In the case of British Telecom and British Gas, which have already been privatised, two steps would need to be taken to offset the risk that they might at some future date abuse their monopoly power. One is to re-examine the regulatory body in order to be sure that it would be strong enough to carry out its tasks and not be subject to regulatory capture. The other would be to examine the extent to which greater competition or liberalisation could be introduced by means of additional licensing, franchising, or an extension of operational contract tendering. In the case of enterprises still under discussion, these aspects should be seriously considered before any appropriate Bills are submitted to Parliament.

The risk is that if these steps are not taken, a future Government with a different political background could claim to have every reason to take these enterprises back into the public sector. Indeed, they would have very little difficulty in doing so because the enterprises would have been maintained in their integrity. On the other hand, a determined and successful effort to liberalise them and introduce more competition into certain parts of their activity, and to retain in public ownership those parts where the competition could not be introduced, might provide a long-term solution on which all political parties could agree.

Assuming that the Government were in a position to continue with the privatisation programme after the next election, there could still come a time when a nucleus of enterprises currently in the public sector could not be privatised. These would largely be enterprises which, for a variety of reasons, would continue to require an injection of public funds. The coal industry is still in the process of restructuring, and the merchant part of the shipbuilding industry remains in difficulty because of the pressure of intense worldwide competition. Although the steel industry is showing improved results, nevertheless it might be some time before these could be regarded as sufficiently profitable to be floated on the market. What is important for those enterprises likely to be left in the public sector is that their objectives and methods of operation should be more clearly defined than in the past, and Government intervention much reduced. One way to do this might be to set up a regulatory body in each case. In the legislation establishing these regulatory bodies, the objectives and methods of operation of each enterprise would be set out. The measures which would need to be taken to ensure that there was no abuse of monopoly position should be stated and any limits on price movements, where appropriate, should also be indicated. In other words, these regulatory bodies would be similar to those which have been set up in the case of the gas and tele-communications industries. The advantage of this arrangement would be to keep Government out of the day-to-day operations with which they have been too prone to get involved in the past.

It is essential to find some way of dealing with the nationalisation/privatisation argument on a definitive basis which could stand the test of time. Alternating policies applied throughout the post-war period have not only been harmful to the public enterprises themselves but also to the rest of the British economy. If the present spate of privatisation were at some future date to be succeeded by a similar spate of renationalisation or socialisation, this would be a most harmful development. What is needed is some basis on which both a public and political consensus can be established. It is suggested that this might be achieved as follows:

(i) Those public enterprises which have been privatised and are in a clearly competitive situation should be left there.
(ii) Those public enterprises which are monopolies and which have been privatised as such should be restructured to

introduce greater competition and liberalisation. Any further privatisation of natural monopolies should only be undertaken within a competitive framework.

(iii)   Those public enterprises likely to be left in the public sector should be provided with a clearer definition of their objectives and methods of operation, and should be distanced from Government by the establishment of appropriate regulatory bodies.

The Argument
for Privatisation

Peter Clarke

> *In every great monarchy of Europe the sale of the crown lands*
> *would produce a very large sum of money, which, if applied*
> *to the payment of the public debts, would deliver from*
> *mortgage a much greater revenue than any which those lands*
> *have ever afforded to the crown . . . When the crown lands*
> *had become private property, they would, in the course of a*
> *few years, become well-improved and well-cultivated . . . It*
> *would in all cases be in the interest of the society to divide the*
> *lands among the people, which could not well be done better,*
> *perhaps, than by exposing them to public sale.*
> Adam Smith, *The Wealth of Nations*, 1776.

Privatisation is an ugly word that describes a wonderful process. The ghosts of the imagination that have haunted capitalism are being exorcised. The degradation and impoverishment attributed by Romantics and Marxists is no longer regarded as the shadow of a free market. The propensity to stagger into depression and unemployment, which seemed the essence of the unplanned economy, is now seen to be the result of too much State control of the money system, not a lack of State power.

The whole spectrum of policies which assumed that the State could be benign, benevolent and competent are dissolving. Nationalised industries have been a tangible failure. A British Rail sandwich seems the distillation of socialist achievement, but it is not just the corporatist inheritance of Herbert Morrison that is challenged by privatisation. The monuments of William Beveridge and Maynard Keynes are visibly corroding in the fresh air of critical intelligence.

I will argue that privatisation is a process that, although it started hesitantly and timidly, in Britain, will capture the world. Even the most crusty socialist states are beginning to nibble at liberal ideas. I will examine how markets allow people to exchange ideas and alternatives through the price structure, and that this is an eighteenth-century ideal only recently rediscovered. I will try to explain why competition is a higgledy-piggledy discovery procedure that is infinitely more adaptive and responsive than any democratic or bureaucratic alternative.

Privatisation registers in most of our imaginations as only a series of advertising exercises which allows the Government to float off its odd portfolio of State corporations to a public happy to be gifted assets at a discount (and often protected by monopoly status such as British Gas, or by biased regulatory advantage such as British Airways).

I will show that there are more than twenty different ways of freeing institutions and people from the cobwebs of the State, and that privatisation will be the technique finally to neutralise all socialist ideas. If liberal politicians (which in our country means Tories) have the flair, they can employ privatisation and deregulation policies to dissolve their political opponents' intellectual coherence and interest group bases.

I will also argue that privatisation opportunities range far beyond auctioning State assets. Schools and health care and pensions can be liberated. Even institutions such as prisons, anciently conceded as State monopolies, should be opened up to market alternatives. These reforms are not about making money, or pursuing efficiency, though that may be their happy by-product. They are about harmonising and opening society. They are about freedom. Privatisation is not an option for accountants; it can be the most thrilling idea to redirect all of politics. It will enhance our material prosperity, in ways that we cannot predict.

As a good British idea should be, privatisation was stumbled upon inadvertently by the Government. A haphazard or accidental funding event has evolved into a quiet crusade to rewin the world for markets. Indeed, the first notable exercise of selling off substantial State assets was accomplished by Dennis Healey when he was Chancellor of the Exchequer. In June 1977, the Labour Government, with its elbows nudged by the IMF, sold 67 million shares in British Petroleum for £564 million. The Treasury's collective consciousness stumbled on the obvious but previously evaded fact that the State had inherited, acquired, expropriated, sequestered, subsidised, borrowed or bought its way into significant holdings of thousands of companies that were nominally private firms. To raise useful sums without raising an old tax or imposing a new one seemed flawlessly attractive to politicians. Selling off the coal mines or the steel industry would be to offend the ancestors of the Labour Party, but auctioning paper shares in an international oil company was blameless.

From this simple urgent necessity a force has gained momentum that will engulf and transform the world. The Communist nations are rediscovering the advantages of markets. By delegating power and responsibility, they are privatising their inert State trading agencies. Peking even has a 'socialist assets exchange' – a stock market. The Third World, lost in a cycle of brutality and poverty, is being taught that interstate aid blocks their future. Private property and land rights are an idea which is only just beginning to liberate the southern hemisphere.

Since 1979, and the election of Mrs Thatcher's first Government, numerous and anomalous firms have been sold from the State to the market. Cable and Wireless, a remnant of imperial telegraphs, has been born again and is now challenging the old Post Office telephone monopoly, which itself was privatised in 1984. British Sugar was one-quarter owned by the Government until 1981. British Road Services, in one of the most aesthetically pleasing privatisation drives, was transformed into the National Freight Corporation as a management and employee buy-out. Associated Port Holdings disappeared from the Treasury in two tranches in 1983 and 1984. British Rail's hotels were sold in 1984. Jaguar Cars was the first element from the miserable and money-eating British Leyland to find its way back into the market. The National Seed Organisation, the Forestry Commission,

British Gas and British Airways have all joined in the most unexpected but popular auction Britain has ever experienced.

The privatisation experiment will prove to be the enduring success of the eight years of Tory government since 1979. Yet there were few plans to open the economy up in either of the manifestos. Ministers were not at ease with the unfamiliar language of privatisation. Edward Heath's Government had lost its interest in privatisation after selling off Thomas Cook's, the travel agent, and a few pubs in Carlisle that Lloyd George had brought into state control in World War I. Beyond this, the Tories' instincts were that it was provocative and pointless to denationalise industries. In their hearts they felt that a successor socialist Government would expropriate the owners again. They dismissed as merely utopian the ideas of Enoch Powell and a few isolated 'extremists' that capitalism could be made so popular that no Labour Government would dare challenge it. The timorousness of the Conservatives under Mr Heath's leadership is the more perplexing as the Labour Party itself was becoming convinced that nationalisation, in the 1945 mould, was unpopular. Anthony Crosland and like-minded socialist politicians shared the view of the American Democrats that regulation and taxation were more effective instruments to achieve equality than direct State ownership.

In the long run, the cowardice or confusion of the 1970–4 Tory administration emboldened just enough of Mr Heath's frustrated colleagues to argue for more adventurous ideas. Sir Geoffrey Howe advanced his idea of enterprise zones. Miniature Hong Kongs – without central or municipal controls – might do more to revive inner city dereliction than permutations of grant-giving agencies with 'regional policies'. Enterprise zones represented a psychological shift beyond the scope of the more modest zones that the Customs and Excise eventually asphyxiated. The regeneration of the derelict landscape of the London Docklands by removing the powers of the local authorities in the East End has been the only tangible result of his theme, but the general political appreciation of the nature of urban development was transformed from something rigidly planned and designed by the State into something more imaginative, devised and created by enterprise. If Enterprise Zones and Freeports with their minimal State regulation and taxes, are a good thing, this invites the question as to why the whole nation could not be made into one. It might be pleasing to keep Sunderland or Liverpool as museums of socialism for the edification and enlightenment of future generations. Building ships which no one wanted with steel no one needed, and corralling workers on soulless council estates, will seem entirely perverse in twenty years' time.

Privatisation started as a rather obscure and technocratic innovation. It was not thought likely to touch people's minds and hearts, let alone their pockets. The initial privatisations were absorbed by City institutions. Only slowly did Ministers realise that it won them not only the affection of stockbrokers and merchant bankers, but the approval of the Treasury and the smile of the Prime Minister; and only years later did they appreciate that privatisation was having a quietly revolutionary effect on the allegiances of the newly enfranchised shareholders.

Mrs Thatcher says she wants to nudge socialism off the stage of British politics. She has been so cautious about opening up the schools and the health system that she has merely kept them miserable on their ever-expanding budgets. In the industrial areas of policy she has successfully marginalised socialism. The very idea of collective ownership of production, distribution and exchange looks stale and uninviting. The atavistic and timeless attractions of socialism – a sense of community and of mutuality – fall back to voluntary associations and cooperative ventures, which use Business Expansion Scheme moneys and create new generations of miniature capitalists. Even the most ancient territory of socialism, the municipal underworld, is being opened up to competitive tendering and subcontracting.

The wave of privatisation that rippled through even to the most protected beaches was caused by the intellectual exhaustion of the idea of socialism and the need of its hungry welfare agencies to eat more money. Only when the schools have been sold off, the Department of Health and Social Security offered as a management buy-out, and the British Medical Association and the Law Society arraigned for restraint of trade, can we be confident that socialism will be safely bequeathed to the archaeology of ideas.

Privatisation was no more than a fairly desperate way of raising money for the Treasury, but it has become a way to inoculate everyone against the conceits of the State by creating us all shareholders with a rentier interest in the market. Privatisation will free the working classes from their servile status as local authority tenants, dragooned into local authority schools and trapped in forlorn, often fictitious, jobs. Freeing the serfs is an honourable adventure, but so far only a very few Tories have had the imagination to see what privatisation could create. Property-owning democracy is a cliché that merely registers thoughts of mortgage tax relief and semi-detached propriety, but with everyone an owner the amount of coercion in society shrivels. Without coercive powers, socialism is dead.

As I write, the Tory party has decided to withdraw the sale of the Water Authorities because it might upset the electorate. The auctioning of British Coal's pits and mines, and the liberalisation of the electricity boards has been abandoned out of a false sense of prudence. The abolition of State pensions in favour of personal private pension arrangements has been dropped, and the civil servants in the Department of Education appear to have diverted the Party from giving purchasing power to every parent through vouchers or grants. The resilience of the conventional enemies of privatisation seems less of a hazard than the timidity and caution of its putative friends. Every Secretary of State, every Minister of State, and every Parliamentary Under-Secretary ought to be jostling to bring forward their departmental plans to liberalise their areas. The first one to scrap his department outright, and leave the papers to the archivists, ought to feel assured of a dukedom.

Privatisation diffuses not only the paper claims to property, it also diffuses knowledge. The Division of Knowledge is more important than the Division of Labour. An industry privatised, even where its monopoly is preserved, is better for the rest of the community because it has to use knowledge far more successfully than was necessary in the mortmain of the State. Markets are information-rich cybernetic systems. Privatisation creates a comparative advantage in knowledge.

The form of knowledge conveyed by privatisation is intimate and personal knowledge of the particular circumstances of time and place. Organisations that dip their toes, even tentatively, in a market, such as British Telecom, become aware of a stream of individual preferences to which they were previously immune. The sudden discovery of a public appetite for many new designs, colours and functions on telephone handsets was unknowable without a market. The profusion of telephone gadgets certainly needs technical ingenuity and skill, but they lay inert and unexplored while the old state monopoly offered us only the three-colour, two-model option. The most useful stream of information opened up by privatisation is, perhaps, not only what people may prefer in terms of design or facilities, but what they do not want. Privatisation includes the freedom to fail. Without the negative feedback, the market system would not be correcting and refining itself in its daily, hourly, individual referenda of price signals.

The case for privatisation is that it allows planning to be done better than in the socialist model of a central coordinating and directing authority or in the fascist model of delegated planning and organisation of industries. Market systems, with firms competing against one another, prove to be much more efficient than any variation of authoritarian ideas. It has proved impossible to put at the disposal of central authorities such as the Treasury or the National Coal Board the sort of economic knowledge which is not only dispersed amongst individuals but itself changes in a constant moving kaleidoscope of preferences and prices.

Privatisation allows lack of success to register. Losses and liquidation are profitable to the system. They are the correcting and adjusting procedures which define where resources of talent and capital should be switched. The pool of products and services in markets permutates daily. In the public service they are starved of data about alternative supplies or requirements. Privatisation makes organisations sensitive to individual preferences.

Macro-economics, with its loyalty to aggregates, finds this impossible to accommodate. By inheriting the entire baggage of Keynesian demand management, and control of sup- posedly homogeneous statistics, the Left has found itself forfeiting its libertarian credentials. In pursuit of a wrong- headed mirage such as the 'Balance of Payments' and the preservation of a fixed price for the State bank's currency, as liberal and open-minded a man as Roy Jenkins found himself forbidding families from taking more than £50 for foreign holidays. Planning through the State always unfolds into such petty tyranny.

Privatisation is a liberating force. The management, workers, suppliers and customers of an institution returned to the market (however compromised) are all opened to new streams of information. If this includes the blunt conclusion that some roles are redundant, or can be displaced by mechanisation, or by imports, this is still good news. The suppression of such data by price controls, protection or subsidies only feeds false information into the vast computing system of the market. The market metaphor of 'The Invisible Hand' is an unhappy one; it is better seen as a personal and mental phenomenon – the result of human interactions, not of human designs.

Humility about how much can be known by an individual, a board, a syndicate of experts or a committee of political appointees leads us back towards favouring markets. Know- ledge, in markets, is always tentative and provisional. It is always being retested through the price system in valuing labour or commodities. These adjustments never approach the fiction of 'perfect competition' invented by neo-classical economics.

F. A. Hayek says that if a single philosopher or economist

had devised a system that could coordinate the intentions of people who have no knowledge of one another, as markets can do, then it would have been hailed as a miracle or marvel of the human mind. Leftists, of every colour, seek 'conscious direction', but markets are not end-seeking orders. A competitive economy has no hierarchy of priorities: it is only an information system, the power and flexibility of which is something of a miracle.

If it seems odd to claim that markets achieve miracles, I can assert confidently that markets achieve far better results than any designed or rational order. The history of civilisation seems to me a solid catalogue of societies with a more refined division of labour and elaborated system of exchanges succeeding those controlled by the caprice of chieftains, princelings, military leaders, or religious and ideological systems that lay claim to some lofty purpose or design. Articulated rules of property, and freedom of exchange of this property (which in industrial societies is primarily a series of paper claims), is a matter of justice and equity. It is a rule of fair conduct that people may exchange, swap and barter freely. Nationalisation is only an attempt to empower politicians and their staffs, not the general population.

The unwanted boggy bits of Germany and Italy flourished into the Dutch and Venetian mercantile republics, and the cold, wet bits of northern England cradled the Industrial Revolution because State power was weak. Civilisations prosper when their information systems – their markets – are more open. Hong Kong and Singapore have neither water nor any natural resources, yet they bubble with prosperity. Brazil, the USSR, Mexico, India and China flounder along through their mixtures of mercantilism and socialism. They have vast natural endowments, but their institutional frameworks hinder commercial vitality.

Competitive markets are valuable expressly because the permutations they throw up are entirely unpredictable and unlike anything that could be conceived by one mind or by a democratic assembly. Competition, which, thanks to privatisation, is again becoming a real force, discovers facts that could not have been uncovered without the trial and error process.

It may seem an odd claim, but competition is analogous to scientific discovery, with every participant in the market expressing or stumbling upon facts hitherto unknown. Every manufacturer is permanently buffered by new information about arrivals in the market, employee turnover, regulations, taxes and supplies. The more adaptive and creative he is, the better the market registers it. Each supermarket is a laboratory testing the direction of customer preferences and the areas of future profit.

Scientific procedure concerns itself with general facts or regularities which repeat themselves, but markets consume particular facts unique to each participant and his or her location in time and place. The value, and therefore the price, of items is quite different for people who are apparently similar. Each individual's choice is moving in a broth of subjectivity. So economics offers no testable predictions about human behaviour, any more than scientific procedure offers predictions about what it will discover. Markets allow abstract orders or patterns to emerge which enable the knowledge of everyone to be enhanced, Competition is cooperative.

The apparent chaos of the commodity market ring, or the anonymous electronic hum of the equity markets, is digesting and interpreting more information, more usefully, than any other method of allocating resources. Socialists scoff at markets, dismissing them as casinos, blind to virtue or long-term perspectives, but markets seem to predict (guess) the future far better than econometric models or planners. Markets are permanently self-correcting processes – never correct, and certainly never perfect, but constantly adapting to new data. Market prices, like scientific ideas, are always provisional.

Serious socialists have begun to yield to the classic argument of Ludwig Mises that economic orders need prices to coordinate activity and to transmit information about relative needs. Socialism had assumed that needs were known and identifiable, and that material resources could be reshaped to meet them. Nationalisation and central planning have shown this to be an error. Privatisation brings the oxygen of knowledge concerning relative cost to the economy.

Socialism is a belief that a nation can be organised towards the achievement of a number of ends. These can be expressed abstractly in terms such as social justice, democracy or equality, but very specific policy prescriptions flow from them. Redistributive tax and welfare structures, the delegation of powers to elected bodies, and the suppression of choice in schooling or housing, is the form nationalisation has always taken.

Liberals do not offer an alternative hierarchy of ends which they think should be pursued, let alone described. A privatisation initiative does not describe how that industry or service should or will evolve. Privatisation is about discovering how the free interplay of everyone will fashion the oil, television, education or book market. The fewer controls and regulations, the more diverse will be the firms and products that emerge. Socialists identify needs that can either be satisfied or unsatisfied. Liberals want to use the knowledge of everyone's circumstance and preference, but not in an organised or stipulated way. The ends of privatisation are individual and contrary. They are unknowable.

There is an apparent paradox that although socialists seek order, design and system, their policies produce chaos, decay and dissolution, while capitalism, eschewing hierarchies or purposes, yet achieves spontaneous order and regularity. The reason, I believe, is that markets are constantly eating information and adapting, while bureaucracy can only suppress information or distort it. Bureaucracy sounds a tendentious word, but this is all that socialism ever offers. Whatever the bright prospect of cooperation and mutual support of the socialist imagination, the reality is always a mixture of British Steel and the Department of Health and Social Security.

Expectations are coordinated by the continual disappointment of other expectations. Market activity is about not buying a thousand alternatives to the one chosen. Privatisation allows a constant and mutual adjustment of the plans of individual households and firms. It also ensures that whatever services or goods are being supplied will be as cheap as possible. A test of this is the very great difficulty in discovering ways of beating present participants in open markets. This is especially true of State enterprises which can never beat private ones without protection by regulation or price fixing. Nationalisation is only the misuse of power amplifying the misuse of resources. Competition is a game of chance and skill, but it is a game where the referee (the State) does not alternate as a player.

All this seems galaxies away from the mundane sale of State assets, but I believe that by including everyone as participants in the market, privatisation will open minds. The material enrichment is secondary to the tactical or psychological damage it is causing the Left in politics.

My two favourite examples of privatisation initiatives being used to short-circuit socialism are drawn from Canada and Chile. In British Columbia the Provincial Government decided to trump critics of its attempts to sell off the 'British Columbian Natural Resources and Investment Corporation', a sort of hybrid of the National Enterprise Board and the Forestry Commission. The Canadian Left, echoing British Labour Party gripes about privatisation with 'Why Buy What You Already Own?' campaigns, prompted the Tory Government in Vancouver to give away the assets of the BCNRIC. Shares were gifted to all adults on the electoral role who applied for their allocation, and new equity was also issued. The Canadian Left were trounced and the sensation of shareholding was extended to the majority of citizens. Some years after its privatisation, the share price slipped, but that merely served to teach the nature of investment. The BCNRIC management performance was closely scrutinised by the entire population, where five years previously they needed only to lobby a few ministers and civil servants for a further subvention.

In Chile President Pinochet's often brutal regime has had some striking success in applying privatisation ideas. In particular, the bloated and bankrupt State pension system was liberated. Chileans were free to nominate different contractors to husband their pension savings. The relative performance of these funds has become a matter of personal and detailed interest, and it checked the old temptation of the Santiago politicians to skim the State insurance system in order to subsidise further commercial follies or military vanities. Chileans learned very quickly how their portfolio managers were faring and, without any of Professor Friedman's books being read, a nation was converted to participatory capitalism.

John Redwood, formerly head of the Policy Unit in Downing Street, has argued that both British Rail and the Central Electricity Generating Board could be used as vehicles for universal sharegiving, emulating the Canadian experience. The morale of their employees could be enhanced by co-ownership of popular shareholdings. In both cases the problem would be the relaxation of Government controls. The commuter interest in assured and cheap trains might contradict the shareholder instinct for greater revenue, and the CEGB interests would quickly fragment into the different functions of generation, grid transmission and the servicing of electric appliances.

My own favourite is the obscure but vast Property Services Agency. This quango operates the unwieldy property empire of the British State, from the Royal Navy's network of squash courts to Mount Pleasant Airport in the Falklands; it also supplies every civil servant with his correct grade of desk, carpet and filing cabinet. Converted into a unit trust and given to every voter who sought an allocation, it would encourage us all to look askance at Governmental mismanagement of resources. Those resources would be run so much more efficiently that we would all be individually enriched by the rising value of our units, while the State's own bookkeeping would be usefully improved. The attraction of such populist devices is not so much the implicit improvement in efficiency as the possibility of breaking the back of the Labour Party. Adam Smith envisaged princes and courtiers as the opponents of privatisation: socialists are heirs to the Stuart ideal of lawless and expense-free powers.

The significance of privatisation is political. The enhanced productivity and flexibility of the industries concerned is a blessing for staff and customers, but the enduring advantage is the subtle change in the political balance. The essential ingredient is the participation of employees through share-discount schemes, and of the general public by allocation procedures. If sufficient people have their own stake in production, distribution and exchange, socialism is dead.

Privatisation often seems to be a wheeze for giving pleasure to ministers, advertising agencies and stockbrokers, but such pleasures wither if the process does not enjoy popularity, measured by ordinary people clamouring for their share allocations. The magical element in the privatisation of the 1980s is this universal participation in the diffusion of shares. Previously they would have been lost in the portfolios of pension funds. Privatisation has become a consumer event. This may be euphoric, but the heavy promotional efforts have had a huge psychological effect. Every advertisement offering Rolls Royce or British Airways or British Gas shares has been a Party political broadcast on behalf of capitalism.

Privatisation has not merely restored ownership to a few anonymous industrialists, but to ordinary individuals at large; and therein lies its attraction. It has been such a success that the very word 'nationalisation' has disappeared from the language of the Parliamentary Labour Party and the socialist intellectuals. Euphemisms such as 'Social Ownership' or 'Ownership by the Community' scarcely hide the embarrassment of the Left. It has been outmanoeuvred by the Conservatives. The fun is increased by the realisation that this happened without any push from Conservative Central Office or from ministers, and that merchant bankers and fund managers all agreed it was impractical and utopian nonsense. The consensus in the City for some years after Mrs Thatcher's election was that privatisation would be limited to the occasional divestment of an NEB firm weaned from its subsidy drip-feed. The City experts declined to believe that the market could absorb a stock the size of BT, British Gas or British Airways. Practical men are usually wrong. It was the combination of evangelism and political chance that imposed privatisation on a reluctant City.

Tories who were reconciled to a graceful surrender to socialism have protested that privatisation represents little more than a hard-pressed household selling off its family silver while continuing to overspend. Yet the subsidy-hungry nationalised industries, although heirlooms, were not assets. The overspending was caused by the unquenchable appetite of the public sector. Privatisation is not the dissipation of resources; it is the unlocking of opportunities.

Until 1983 I would have been happy to nominate council house sales as the most successful privatisation initiative, and the one most subversive to socialism; but the creation of one and a half million BT shareholders, including 220,000 BT staff, who had previously held no shares, seems a more important symbol of the future defeat of socialist ideals than the break-up of local authority empires. The reform would have been more happy had BT been split into different companies jostling for the telephone traffic, and had Oftel not been created to block new entrants into the telecommunications market. Yet these reservations seem sanctimonious compared to the popular pleasure in holding their little wodge of shares.

Even after privatisation, BT and British Gas have preserved their monopoly; and the same will doubtless apply to the Electricity Council. I believe this was a tactical error by the politicians responsible. Directory Enquiries would answer and gas engineers would keep their appointments if they were private contractors to a more open system. Dispersal of the shares was the main benefit of privatisation with monopoly. Oftel and Ofgas (and presumably Ofspark) run a permanent risk of regulatory capture by the monopoly they are meant to police. It would be easier and better for the self-respect of privatisation if competition were opened up.

Opponents of privatisation have argued that the terms and conditions of employment offered after privatisation are, or will be, poorer than under State control. Certainly privatisation will bring a rapid contraction in numbers employed, and a swift reform of antique restrictive practices; but the prospects for employees in organisations removed from the State sector would seem to be enhanced. The important element of the market status is that they have to satisfy customers. Security of tenure may please trade unions, but it motivates nobody.

Employee shareholders in companies removed from public ownership do not enjoy workers' democracy or anything like the participatory ideals of syndicalist socialism. They forfeit the near-security of tenure that so often accompanies public agencies. Yet as employees with a modest stake in their firm, they become alert to waste and incompetence. They become participants.

The millionth council house was sold to its previous tenant family in 1986. That means that the independence and self-respect of one million households has been enhanced. The notional value of such homes, now enhanced by domestic improvements, is of no importance in the GDP statistics, but of vital importance to each family involved. Tory targeting must move on to free the remaining serfs locked into dependence on municipal landlords in their flats and tower blocks. I believe that dynamite may prove to be the best option for some of these grim concrete monuments to socialism; but transformed into housing associations, tenant cooperatives, or sold to private developers freed from rent controls, even the most gaunt and bleak council block could be converted into comfortable and attractive homes. The Tories have thus far enjoyed the discomfort of the Labour municipal lords, but they have not tapped an authentic seam of anger at what 'the party of working people' has imposed on so many families. Privatisation is bringing a massive switch of resources away from the State (which means bureaucrats and politicians) to the people. The popular potential of this accidental revolution is still surprising Tory ministers who had seen their careers as largely absorbed in accommodating socialism.

Dr Madsen Pirie is the leading exponent of the 'public choice' school of economics in the UK. He argues that privatisation is not a single solution to be applied to every case of a public-sector body, but sees it as a process for discovering creative and innovative solutions to the decay or inertia of the state. Dr Pirie identifies twenty-one different methods of dissolving socialism with minimal pain. They are:

1. SELLING THE WHOLE CONCERN. There are always occasions when the State's involvement in any area of expertise can be fused into a single unit and sold. Amersham International PLC was previously the disparate interest of the government in radionics and man-made radioactivity and scientific instruments. It was offered for sale in 1982, and realised a price of £70 million. Previously this had only incurred costs.

2. SELLING SEPARATE PARTS OF THE CONCERN. Smaller organisations that have lived under the protection of larger State concerns, such as British Rail's Sealink Services or Wytch Farm Oilfield of the Gas Board, were sold with minimal friction. By opening to market disciplines they will either grow or atrophy. Both are good for the economic interest.

3. SELLING PROPORTIONS OF THE WHOLE OPERATION. It may not be necessary, and may even be prudent, to sell only a percentage of a State concern. Britoil, having been made legally into a company, sold 51% of its shares. Associated British Ports and British Aerospace adopted this technique with apparent success. The fact that Britoil was under-subscribed does not compromise the success of the sale. The underwriters ensured the sum sought. The promise of sale seems to have a radicalising effect on managers.

4. SELLING TO THE WORKFORCE. Selling a company to its workers is one of the simplest ways of weaning people from socialism. Worker-owners seem to see the world differently from employees with only a wage interest. The National Freight Corporation is regarded as the most successful model of this technique, but the key ingredient remains the ambition

of the managers. Victualic, the British Steel pipe subsidiary, was sold to 630 of its 885 workers. The psychological transformation was vivid, as was the rise in share price.

5. *GIVING TO THE PUBLIC.*   The British Government has not yet been bold enough to try a gift of a public-sector institution to the population. Although the sheer size of the electoral roll is intimidating, I believe that the Forestry Commission, with the preponderance of its notional assets in Scotland, could be gifted to every Scottish family – 'their wee bit hill and glen', as envisaged by the SNP anthem.

BT shares were offered with vouchers and discounts to telephone subscribers. It worked as a magnet. Outright gifting should be employed with the rail or electricity industry. The UK stocks of the EEC-induced food mountains could be gifted to each household, affording popular pleasure and public saving.

6. *GIVING TO THE WORK-FORCE.*   In 1984 the workers of the Channel hovercraft services, previously owned by BR, sold its assets for £1 million to a staff consortium. Gifting will be most attractive when the assets seem least capable of revitalisation. I regard coal mines as perfect models for gifting to the miners. They would be freed from centuries of direction by owners and union officials. Miner-owners would cause Mr Scargill's lingering influence to evaporate. I think the productivity of pits would soar, as well as the self-respect of the mineworkers.

7. *CHARGING FOR THE SERVICE.*   Dental, optical and medical prescription charges are a way of part-removing expenditure and expertise from direct State control. Libraries, museums, swimming pools, opera and theatre would reorientate themselves to suit consumer preferences if they had to respond to price data. There is a subtle but powerful process which assures discounted costs for primarily middle-class diversions. Pricing stops this cross-subsidisation.

8. *CONTRACTING-OUT TO PRIVATE BUSINESS.*   Local Government functions such as refuse collection, pest control,

street cleaning, school meals, catering or laundering, legal and accounting functions and even core administrative roles can all be contracted out by State agencies rather than be done directly by them. Ideally, private single-operator monopolies should not merely succeed public monopolies. Different contracting firms could clean different streets. Academic studies of sub-contracting suggest savings of one-third, but they cannot calibrate the enhanced profit of workers' morale. Unpopular duties such as wheel-clamping can be tendered out to mitigate a department's public relations sensitivities.

9. *DILUTING THE PUBLIC SECTOR.* By permitting private contractors to share the funding and risk, investment can be accelerated without the State's budget being diverted. The entire friction over the lack of 'infrastructure spending' would have been neutralised if civil engineers were allowed to toll for road or sewer repair. The participation of Trafalgar House in building the new bridge and tunnel over and under the Thames was delayed until the company took the contracted risk. Council estates could all be shared with private developers or demolition contractors.

10. *BUYING OUT EXISTING INTEREST GROUPS.* The opponents to reform can be paid to yield their privilege; but it is simpler to curtail their numbers by blocking entry. Thus the lobby for retaining rent controls is withering as new tenant/landlord agreements escape the hazards of the Rent Acts. Many coalminers have been effectively bought out of their pit employment by generous redundancy payments, so dissolving the power of the NUM as an interest group.

11. *SETTING UP COUNTER-INTEREST GROUPS.* Countervailing interest groups can be nurtured to dissolve the past. The alternative miner's union fostered in 1985 is an example of this technique. The interest shown by council house tenants in acquiring the 70% capital gift of the value of their homes has created a new lobby that has almost intimidated the Labour Party away from its opposition to municipal sales.

12. DEREGULATION THROUGH VOLUNTARY ASSOCI-ATIONS. Regulation through private intermediary bodies such as Lloyds allows the State to limit its control of the insurance markets. The inspection of building and construction sites can be done by trade bodies instead of local authorities. Voluntary or philanthropic provisions can flourish if their charity or tax status is enhanced.

13. ENCOURAGING ALTERNATIVE BODIES. Private bodies directly competing with State concerns can cast new light on the efficiency of ancient public sector habits. The cheeky creation in 1976 of the University of Buckingham, with its two-year degree courses, is already jolting State-sector universities such as Aberdeen to rethink their organisations.

14. MAKING SMALL-SCALE TRIALS. Enterprise zones and freeports have served as models which are being copied in wider forms.

15. REPEALING OR RELAXING MONOPOLY STATUS. The relaxation of the controls on long-distance coaches has been an unchallenged success. The regulations turn out to have been entirely superfluous, hindering good, quick transport for people on more modest incomes. The removal of the powers of traffic commissioners to control urban buses is now being tried, but would be even more popular if the local monopoly of taxi-cartels were also dissolved.

16. ENCOURAGE EXIT FROM STATE PROVISION. If the per capita cost of the NHS could be deducted from family tax bills on condition they were invested in comprehensive health insurance policies, the pressure on the NHS and the politicians would be entirely different. The growth of private and personal pensions as an alternative to the State pension has surprised all the actuaries.

17. EMPLOY VOUCHERS. If the State has to guarantee schooling (though I cannot see why), it does not actually have to provide the schooling. If every family had a voucher equivalent to the DES's per capita expenditure, they could redeem it at the school which they thought appropriate. Socialists comfort themselves that ordinary working people would only be confused by the profusion of choice that teachers would offer. The Left will look lame trying to disenfranchise people given such purchasing power.

18. *CURBING STATE POWERS.* The State has accrued hundreds of powers to inspect, regulate and enter businesses. These can be relaxed or abolished, but the authority of State agencies, especially regional 'development' funds to buy into companies, can be blocked. The Welsh Development Agency or the Highlands and Islands Development Board powers are easily limited.

19. *DIVESTMENT.* Past acquisitions of companies can be divested with obvious ease. Since 1979 the Government has sold its holding in an average of twenty firms a year.

20. *LIQUIDATION.* Bankruptcy procedures can be appropriate for liquidating unnecessary institutions. Teacher-training colleges have been subject to similar processes, and twenty-seven hospitals have been put through processes analogous to liquidation. As a piece of political showmanship, liquidation could be useful.

21. *ALLOW PRIVATE SUBSTITUTION.* A number of functions exercised by quangos have been abolished. Disappearance of the quangos causes little public distress. The main misgiving about the abandonment of so many boards, councils, trustees, advisory panels, agencies and committees is that they cramp political powers of patronage.

Madsen Pirie's list of options includes some that have scarcely been tried and others whose success is so clear and acclaimed that even the socialists are having to yield. Privatisation is a micro-political method of dissolving socialism far beyond the range of the traditional nationalised corporations.

Professor Pedro Schwartz, of the University of Madrid, wittily and truthfully declares that 'the private sector is that part of the economy controlled by the State: the public sector is that part controlled by nobody'. It is privatisation which, through alternatives, is reopening the public sector to the influence of customers.

Intermittent attempts have been made to improve public sector institutions. Unless this includes bringing them back to the market, the reforms all peter out. Efforts to improve the performance of nationalised bodies are a waste of energy, not because people in the public sector are especially slothful or inept but because the very idea of the State as an economic agency misunderstands the advantages of voluntary exchange over coerced distribution.

Efficiency drives which try to apply private enterprise expertise to nationalised bodies have generated handsome contracts for management consultancies and have even brought a few knighthoods and peerages, but any time-and-motion studies or inventory improvements are tokens against the brutal fact that competition is not present. Monopoly is a licence to snooze.

Such drives to enhance efficiency can have a marginal and short-lived effect, but the institutions themselves do not have to respond to customer dissatisfaction or to competitors' new prices or services. Similarly, occasional drives to eliminate waste are worthy but futile attempts to pretend that the public-sector body is subject to the same real discipline of failure. Independent analysts can identify flagrant abuses and impose better stock control, but it is a system lacking in information, without penalty and reward. Temporary results are won from auditing, but they are very modest.

Even more thankless are efforts to identify and cut out unwanted operations. However inefficient or little used some services may be, the public friction created by attempts to end them are out of proportion to the savings. Not only do the staff complain, they will nurture lobbies for retaining facilities even when they are scarcely used. There is no career advantage to any public servant in pinpointing and eliminating unused railway services, libraries, laboratories, or offices.

Imposing budget ceilings either on departments of State

or nationalised industries only concentrates funds to the elements with the greatest political sensitivity or clout. Savings will often be made not by cutting the least productive units but by paring back the services with most public appeal. This generates a good rumpus about the misanthropic 'cuts'. Cash limits only accelerate the public sector's ability to make wrong decisions. What the public will tolerate is different from what the public would buy.

The prospectus of socialism, which successfully won the political agenda from all parties one hundred years ago, was that the State could organise resources and production for the general good. The apparent enrichment of the capitalist at the expense of labour would be reversed. Experience has shown that it was the nations with the greater degree of free markets that prospered. Privatisation is the word that describes the process that has won back the future for capitalism.

Nationalisation is an attempt to deal with problems by large size and detailed controls: privatisation favours smaller units and minimal controls. Privatisation is a micro-political idea. Its strength is that it is the best way for people to free themselves from the clamour of those who administer the State, those who work for nationalised bodies, and those special interests who seek benefits from State or municipal agencies. Privatisation neutralises or converts these special interests, merging them with the general interest as defined through the market.

The sale of British Gas was more than the largest stock market flotation in history. It converted the animosity of the senior managers, who became directors; and the employees were magnetised by generous share offers, some free, some at a discount through wage deductions. The general public were attracted by the advertising and sales campaign. Yet four years previously the simple attempt to privatise the gas showrooms had floundered through the hostility and fear of managers, workers and customers. Some even argue that the conventionally 'wet' Energy Minister, Peter Walker, was personally converted to the political case for privatisation as a vote-winner.

The thrill of the more successful privatisation initiatives is the switching of the allegiance of workers by participation in operations through their new status as shareholders. The National Freight Corporation is the most striking example of this technique, but British Telecom and British Airways have demonstrated the collapse of trade union or staff opposition by buying out their interest in inertia.

Privatisation need not be a matter of confrontation or friction. Properly applied, its optional applications can circumvent or bypass resistance. Notions of what is politically possible or practical are radically different after patient efforts to implement micro-political ideas. I believe that nothing now done by the State could not be more successfully done by the market.

The preservation, almost intact, of the monopoly status of some firms is a shortcoming. I doubt that the solution lies in regulatory agencies which, in the case of British Telecom or British Gas, will lead to collusion and circumvention. The best prospect for the future is to allow free entry of new suppliers at the margin of these gigantic firms. Small tele-communications and gas companies could eat into the market share of these giants by simply charging lower tariffs.

A private monopoly forfeits the political power to catch the ear both of civil servants and politicians. Its primary relation-ships are with customers, suppliers and shareholders, not with political patrons. It can raise its funds and deploy its resources on commercial grounds, not subject to the geog-raphy of marginal constituencies or other political caprices.

Technical innovation cannot be suppressed as is possible in a State corporation. The old Post Office telephone mono-poly has rapidly been compromised by the cellular radio phones introduced by several companies.

Privatisation permits institutional change to happen piecemeal. Evolution is eased and accelerated by free markets. Industries can learn and adapt peacefully where public sector bodies can only preserve old patterns or consume capital.

Future applications of privatisation include schools, pen-sions, legal services, prisons and care of the old. F. A. Hayek, the philosopher with the best paternity claim to all the competing schools of privatisation, nominates the central powers of the State bank as the crucial target for liberalisation. His essay 'The Denationalisation of Money' challenges the assumption we all make (and on which Keynesian socialists depend) that the minting and printing of currency is best done solely by the State.

The privatisation of currency, whereby coexistent forms of money competed for use, would resolve or dissolve problems contrived by State policy. Balance of payments questions would have no meaning. The notion of the 'money supply' would be revealed as a mirage. Most important, the very possibility of inflation would evaporate because people's need for money that appreciated and depreciated (debtors versus borrowers) would balance in a stable unit of account.

The waves of depression and unemployment that often have seemed endemic to capitalism would cease. Business cycles, the product of State manipulation of credit, could not occur. Privatised money would inhibit the growth of State expenditure, but its primary attraction would be the breaking of international barriers to the free movement of people, money and resources. Free currencies would liberate people from the subtle oppression of exchange rates and exchange controls. Once again the case for markets is the blessing of freedom as much as efficiency.

In the gold standard we had a universal money which politicians could not touch. For two centuries it integrated the world economy in an unprecedented way. If nations and their central banks ceased to waste their treasure on exchange-rate and interest-rate juggling, the world would be much richer. It is neither a technicality, nor fanciful, to imagine a privatised money system. It is difficult to calculate or guess the advantages that would unfold; but as a device to remove State privilege, it is unmatched.

The benefits of privatisation will be beyond our dreams. Products and services unknown today will evolve and emerge through the market. The victory we need is one of imagination. The old politics is withering. Markets are displacing the illusions of democracy or equality. Within ten years all industrial State ownership will have dissolved: and in the next twenty years human services will be fully engaged and freed.

The remaining size of the public sector defines the opportunities for privatisation. Brutality, ignorance, poverty, corruption and waste – the constant qualities of socialism – can and will be vanquished. The State can be defeated.

Endpiece

Julia Neuberger

> There is . . . little doubt that from the public interest point of view,
> the effectiveness of privatisation both in increasing efficiency and
> promoting the national interest depends on the combination of a
> change in ownership and the maintenance of market pressures
> on management.
>
> Prof. Sir James Ball, *London Business School Journal*, Winter 1986.

The argument about privatisation is more political than
economic. It turns on beliefs about the role of the State and the
desirability of different economic systems which form the
very foundations of political thought. Inevitably it depends
more on questions of value than on questions of fact.

This is well illustrated by one small example from the
essays in this book. It is common ground between John
Rentoul, who argues the case against privatisation, and Peter
Clarke, who argues in favour, that the contracting-out of
publicly provided services has caused some of these to be
eliminated or closed down. The facts are not seriously in
dispute. The difference is in the interpretation. John Rentoul
sees it as a reduction in democratic control which allows the
profit motive to override the needs of the population. Peter
Clarke justifies it as the curtailment of services which were
unwanted; far from accepting that the market overrides the
wishes of the public, he argues that the market permits the
public to get the services that it really wants.

While one can test some of the more extravagant claims
against past experience, it is unlikely that this kind of
argument will be resolved by a careful and impartial study of
the evidence. Even admitting there may be good reason for
certain allegations, such as low productivity in some national-

ised industries, or unacceptably low standards of provision in some contracted-out services, the response might well be that things would otherwise have been worse or that the problems would have been avoided had the underlying policy been better implemented. However, detailed consideration of the arguments of protagonists will help the reader to weigh the comparative merits of the views propounded.

The debate is by no means static; contrary to appearances, both sides do listen to the other and draw some conclusions from experience. The proposals put forward now are different from those advanced forty years ago, but the fundamental differences in value and ideology have not narrowed. The Labour Party, for example, has distanced itself to some degree from the original blueprint of nationalisation, the public corporation, on which the major policy decisions of 1945–51 were based. Whilst retaining its fundamental concern to provide an acceptable level of service for everyone and to emphasise the need for Governmental control of key aspects of the economy, it has recognised that the traditional national-ised industry has sometimes been too 'monolithic' and remote both from its customers and its employees.

Nor have Conservatives gone as far as much of their rhetoric suggests. The privatisation of British Gas and British Telecom has not truly 'set the market free' to operate with all the benefits which Peter Clarke would expect to see flowing from such a move. It is true that these enterprises are now owned by shareholders rather than by the State, though, ironically, with the State retaining a majority share. But they are near-monopolies, regulated far less by competition and the market than by public regulatory authorities with wide powers to set terms and conditions on prices and levels of service.

Quite apart from all this, the nature of the debate has changed dramatically since the Conservatives won power in 1979. Previously the debate was between 'nationalisation' and 'denationalisation'. The issue was whether key industries should be publicly owned or not. The intellectual initiative was with the proponents of nationalisation who argued that the State needed to control the commanding heights of the economy to ensure that they were run in the national interest. Their opponents rested heavily on the claim that nationalised industries were inefficient and unresponsive to their customers' needs.

Today the debate lies between 'privatisation' and 'social ownership'. The change in the terms is far more than cosmetic. First, the proponents of privatisation have taken the initiative, arguing fervently for the superiority of market-based over administered or planned systems. Peter Clarke exemplifies this view when he says that 'competition . . . is infinitely more adaptive and responsive than any democratic or bureaucratic alternative'. The dropping of the essentially negative term 'denationalisation' for the more positive and aggressive term 'privatisation' is an indication of this, just as the adoption of 'social ownership' indicates a certain desire by the Labour Party to distance itself from nationalised industries in their traditional form.

The second important change is that the scope of the debate has widened enormously. If the market has such marvellous properties, it is both natural and logical to extend it to the whole range of State activity. 'Privatisation' covers not only selling the nationalised industries to private share-holders, but also contracting-out services which have been the responsibility of Central or Local Government, or other public bodies. Thus local authorities still ensure that dustbins are emptied and the cost paid out of public revenues, but the actual work is to be carried out under contract by contractors who compete with one another. This logically extends to the idea that schools and hospitals should also be privatised, although this meets with strong political resistance even in the Conservative Party. Other areas in which the idea of privatisation has had an impact are housing, where large numbers of local authority dwellings have been sold to their tenants, and pensions, where the Government has announced measures which are designed to give individuals greater control over their own pension provisions, at least in part.

Where then does privatisation stop? Peter Clarke says: 'The

remaining size of the public sector defines the opportunities for privatisation.' Does this mean that the debate will in future cover the privatisation of the armed forces, the police and the law courts? Probably not, though conceivably the debate will continue to spread as more proposals are developed to bring market forces to play in the provision of public services.

Just as the scope of privatisation has broadened, so too have the arguments used by its opponents. John Rentoul points out that there have been cuts in wage levels, in terms and conditions of service in jobs – most particularly in the contracted-out public services, although employees in privatised companies have suffered as well. He argues that:

> 'even a monetarist has to ask why the pay of the already very low paid and vulnerable should be reduced simply to obtain a marginal reduction in taxes or Government borrowing – at a time when there are so many other items of spending which could be cut, like subsidies to farmers.'

But his critique of privatisation goes further than the consequences for the work-force. He takes issue with the view that the market can be relied upon to offer a more efficient service which meets the needs of the public. Rather he sees it as a mechanism for exploiting the work-force, and offering financial benefits to City institutions, private contractors and a few rich individuals at the cost of lower efficiency, lower standards of provision and diminished democratic control.

The conflict in political values which underlies the privatisation debate is crucial. The implication for those with the responsibility of running public or privatised services, and indeed for the public as a whole, is not comforting. As one administration succeeds another, one can foresee a succession of privatisations and renationalisations which cannot be good for the country, whatever view is taken of the basic issue. One can derive some comfort from the experience following the great wave of nationalisations in the late 1940s. Despite strong rhetoric about nationalisation and denationalisation, there was little move over the following thirty years by either Labour or Conservative when in office to make radical changes in the boundaries of the public sector. There were a number of changes in structure and organisation, for example the splitting of the electricity supply industry and the amalgamation of the gas industry, but these were motivated by more pragmatic considerations. Similar changes have also occurred in industries in the private sector. The main changes explicitly motivated by more political considerations were the denationalisation and subsequent renationalisation of the steel industry, and the nationalisation of the shipbuilding and aerospace industries. If some stability is to return in future, there will be a need for the development of a consensus on some middle course.

Lord Ezra, in his essay, examines that possible middle course at least for the nationalised industries. He recognises that the debate 'has been primarily a political argument, the confrontation of divergent dogmas', and he goes on to argue:

> The continued change in the ownership and organisation of large-scale enterprises in the basic sector of industry has undoubtedly been one of the factors leading to lower economic growth in Britain than in other European countries in the post-war period.

The arguments he puts forward deserve detailed examination and should be contrasted with the positions adopted in the other two essays. At this stage it is worth noting that the polarisation of the debate does not necessarily force one to adopt an extreme position; there is a middle way which gives weight to both of the 'divergent dogmas', and which pays regard to the very different circumstances of the various candidates for privatisation or social ownership.

But let us first examine the history of the debate to show how we have reached the present situation.

Historical Overview

It is essential to give some brief account of the birth and growth of the nationalised industries up until 1979 when the present Conservative administration came to power. The subsequent history is well covered in Lord Ezra's essay.

A convenient starting-point is the year 1918 when the Labour Party adopted a new constitution, which stated their objective as being:

> To secure for the producers by hand or brain the full fruits of their industry, and the most equitable distribution thereof that may be possible, upon the basis of the common ownership of the means of production, and the best obtainable system of popular administration and control of each industry and service.

Clause IV of the Labour Party constitution was not drafted in an intellectual vacuum. It was much influenced by the Marxist and Socialist critique of capitalism, which saw the latter as a fundamentally wasteful system exploiting the workforce to the benefit of the owners of capital. There were a number of distinct strands in the argument, which are reflected in the drafting of this clause.

One strand was the notion of workers' control which found its expression in the form of guild socialism. The idea was that major industries should be jointly managed by the workers and the Government, the latter representing the interests of consumers. A related idea was that of consumer cooperatives. These had been tried and found successful in retailing but had never spread to the manufacturing industries. A second, and ultimately far more important view was that centralised planning and control were necessary to avoid the wasteful duplication of resources which occurred under a competitive system, and to ensure adequate levels of investment. The supporters of this school of thought pointed to the success of the centralised planning of industry during World War I (repeated in a much more far-reaching way in

World War II), and later to the problems brought about by fragmentation, under-investment and bad labour relations in the coal industry and the railways. The depression of the 1930s further strengthened the views of those who argued that the capitalist system was unable to prevent the hardship and waste of unemployment and under-used industrial capacity. They drew intellectual support for State intervention in industry from the publication in 1936 of Keynes's influential book, The General Theory of Employment, Interest and Money.

By 1918 the State was already heavily involved in trading operations. The Post Office could trace its origins back to the sixteenth century and the telephone service was taken over in 1912. Up to 1933, the Post Office was run like any other Government department, though over the next thirty years there was a series of changes which led to it becoming a public corporation akin to the other nationalised industries. Local authorities also influenced greatly the workings of municipal gas and electricity companies from the end of the nineteenth century.

Although the Labour Party never gained a sufficiently large Parliamentary majority between the wars to put its ideas of public ownership into practice, State involvement in industry proceeded apace on largely pragmatic grounds, with Conservative Governments contributing to the process. Thus the BBC was nationalised in 1926 because of the need to establish an impartial source of public information. A Central Electricity Board was established the following year to ensure coordinated planning and control of the national electricity generation and transmission system. The London Passenger Transport Board was set up in 1933 with control over all London's buses, trams, railways and tubes. In the latter two cases it was widely recognised that a monopoly was necessary to ensure proper coordination and planning; there seems to have been relatively little controversy over the form of implementation as a publicly owned semi-independent Public Service Board.

The Labour Party came to power in 1945 on the basis of a manifesto which called for the public ownership of the fuel and power industries, inland transport and iron and steel. The promised benefits included economies of scale, modernisation of production methods, higher safety standards (for the coal mines), lower charges, and coordination between related industries. There was little hint here either of securing for workers in the industries 'the full fruits of their industry' or of using the nationalised industries to achieve major changes in the economy as a whole.

The form which the Government gave the nationalised industries reflected this emphasis on efficiency and planning. They were not set up as Government departments but as public corporations, with the general duty of breaking even. Although their Boards were appointed by Government, they were statutory bodies with duties laid down by Parliament. The Boards were not representative; Board members were required to act in such a way as to further the aims of the Corporation, as laid down by statute, rather than to pursue the interests of particular groups. The Nationalisation Acts did give ministers the power to issue directions, but the formal nature of these directions suggested that the Government intended to leave the Boards with considerable independence. Subsequently, under both Conservative and Labour administrations, the Government did in fact intervene extensively in the affairs of the nationalised industries, as Lord Ezra's essay makes clear.

The role of the work-force in the running of the industries was also a long way from the hopes and expectations of those who cherished the idea of workers' control. Each industry had a duty to establish mechanisms for joint consultations with their unions on matters affecting the industry at large. But this was never seen or used as a means of giving real control to the work-force.

The main nationalisations carried out by the Attlee administration in 1945–51 were the Bank of England; the National Coal Board (now British Coal); two new airlines which were subsequently amalgamated with the British Overseas Airways Corporation to form British Airways (now privatised); the British Electricity Authority (which after several reorganisations became the Central Electricity Generating Board and twelve Area Boards, with separate Boards for Scotland); the Area Gas Boards (later amalgamated into the British Gas Corporation, and now privatised); and the Iron and Steel Corporation (denationalised in 1953, and renationalised as the British Steel Corporation in 1967). A British Transport Commission was also set up to coordinate all inland transport – rail, road haulage, buses, docks and canals. Its history was the most tortuous of all the nationalised industries; following many reorganisations, there were, after 1968, separate bodies responsible for different forms of transport, notably British Rail, the National Freight Company (now privatised), the National Bus Company (also privatised) and a variety of regional Passenger Transport Executives.

By the end of the Attlee administration, the public trading sector constituted an important part of the economy. It had effective control of transport, fuel and power and the steel industry, as well as of the postal service and telephones. If we add services such as health, education, sewage, water and waste disposal, as well as the law, order and national security, it is evident that the size of the public sector and its power were enormous. In 1960, one quarter of the labour force was directly employed in the public sector, split roughly equally between the nationalised industries, Central Government and the local authorities. The individual industries themselves were large; after nationalisation, the Coal Board, for example, had 700,000 employees. The public sector also had enormous influence indirectly through its purchasing power from the private sector.

It is not possible here to give a balanced account of how the various nationalised industries performed over the next thirty years. There were recurring arguments about wages policy, efficiency, investment, closures and purchasing policy. As Lord Ezra puts it:

> Successive Governments have intervened in their operations for reasons of general policy, thus inhibiting them from conducting their affairs as effectively as might otherwise have been the case.

But one can turn the issue round. Given the enormous concentration of power in the hands of the nationalised industries, how could any Government leave their Boards to determine the national interest and the best means of securing it? The answer in the original statutes was clear; ministers could appoint Boards and give them directions. The Boards would then decide and implement the appropriate course of action in the light of their statutory duties and the specific reserve powers retained by Government. In practice, however, and in the absence of a clear consensus even within any administration, let alone between succeeding administrations, of the balance to be struck between competing priorities – commercial, regional, employment, social service and industrial – such a separation of functions seems Utopian.

One example may illustrate the point. Following the renationalisation of the steel industry in 1967, the British Steel Corporation engaged in a lengthy process of planning how to meet the increased demand it foresaw for steel against the background of an industry which had far less modern plant and substantially lower productivity than its overseas competitors. By 1971 it had formulated a plan based on a production increase from 25 million tonnes to 42 million tonnes over the following decade. The plan involved investment of £11,000 million and the closure of a large number of small plants. Given the implications of this plan for the taxpayer, steel users and regional employment, it is inconceivable that any administration would be prepared to leave such decisions to the BSC Board. After much discussion, the plan was somewhat scaled down and approved. But with the return of a Labour administration in 1974, and the rise in unemployment over the period, the closures were again subject to review. It does not seem surprising that a Government greatly concerned about the loss of jobs in areas where unemployment was already high should be unwilling to leave judgements about the balance between these and commercial considerations to an appointed Board. Without wanting to be wise after the event, one can at least point out that the commercial considerations which inevitably weigh heavily with the Board of a nationalised industry turned out to be far less clear-cut or even well-founded than was represented at the time.

Further examples could be given from the other national-ised industries. For politicians of all persuasions, the urge to use the power of the industries to pursue wider political concerns must have been near-irresistible. For Labour administrations, with a belief in national planning, it was part of the reason for nationalisation. Even for Conservative administrations, the case against intervention was not as strong as might appear; these corporations were not subject to the threat of take-over, competition was generally absent or limited, and they did not need to satisfy the capital markets to raise more funds. There was a perennial suspicion that the Boards were more concerned with grandiose plans for expansion or the avoidance of confronting their employees than with efficiency or meeting the needs of their customers.

This brief overview of the history of nationalisation brings us to 1979, when the present Conservative administration embarked on its privatisation plans. These are well described by Lord Ezra. We now turn to examine in more detail the arguments put forward for and against privatisation.

The Issues

The case for privatisation rests first and foremost on the virtues of the free market, the appeal of which is seen as both political and economic. In a free market, it is argued, the consumer is king. If producers are unwilling to meet people's needs, or if they do so inefficiently, then others will come to take their place. No producers have power as of right to do what they want: they must respond to the customer or perish. This way, the argument runs, free markets are much more efficient than any planned economy can be. They avoid the abuses of power and coercion inherent in any socialist or fascist economy. This point is made by Peter Clarke.

The economic case for free markets rests on a set of economic propositions which is often associated with the eighteenth-century economist, Adam Smith. These ideas have been developed and articulated most recently by economists such as Milton Friedman or F. A. Hayek. Given a number of far-reaching assumptions, it can be demonstrated that a free market will lead to the most efficient allocation of resources in the sense that one can only improve the lot of some people by reducing the circumstances of others.

There are a number of economic criticisms of the free-market philosophy. Firstly, economic efficiency may not be the sole or overriding goal. One important possible alternative aim may be the pursuit of equality or equity. So, for example, economic efficiency may dictate that, in the age of cheap road travel, railways should be confined to a few inter-city routes and bulk freight transport. But somebody who considers it important that people who live in the country and do not have access to cars should be able to travel freely and cheaply by rail may find the free-market solution wholly unacceptable.

Secondly, there are several industries which appear to be natural monopolies. The economics of electricity supply, say, or domestic telephone services, dictate that there should only be one supplier, at least locally. Yet if the market is unregulated the choice is either between many competing suppliers, which would be inefficient, or a single privately owned monopoly. Yet in keeping with the free-market philosophy of maximising profits, a private monopoly would be able to charge higher prices and offer poorer services than customers would wish. So a free market cannot automatically protect consumers against natural monopolies.

A third objection to the free-market philosophy is based on the notion of public property. In a free-market economy, people may well build on green-belt land. Although most of them probably favour green spaces around their cities, the market economy allows no means of paying for such a public benefit; and what is not paid for is not cherished.

Most free marketeers accept the need for some kinds of intervention, such as taxation and social security to redistribute wealth, regulation to split up or control monopolies, and laws to protect public property. But they retain a strong preference for market solutions. By contrast, those who argue for more public ownership lay heavy stress on what they see as the inherent faults of a market system – particularly the gap between the haves and the have-nots, the exploitation of monopoly power by private corporations, and the way in which public interests are in practice ignored by private commercial interests. The citizen in the middle needs to draw his or her own conclusions. Is a British Rail sandwich the distillation of socialist achievement, as Peter Clarke puts it so decisively, or is it merely a small blemish on the face of the nationalised industries which could be removed by a more imaginative Board, less cramped by a tight-fisted Government? Are the examples, listed by John Rentoul, of shoddy services provided by private contractors the inevitable consequences of running public services for private profit, or are they one-off failures which could be dealt with by replacing contractors or rewriting specifications?

If we leave the high ground of general economic theory and examine the area where privatisation has actually been applied, we face a number of much more pragmatic issues. It may be worth distinguishing between three broad areas of privatisation:

1. The privatisation of public monopolies (British Gas, British Telecom).

2. The disposal of non-monopoly trading companies (e.g. Cable and Wireless, British Airways and Amersham International).

3. The contracting-out of public services which continue to be paid for by Central or Local Government.

As Lord Ezra points out the monopolies have been privatised intact; little has been done to break their monopoly power. Public control through ownership has been replaced by licensing and regulation. It remains to be seen what effects this will have.

It is argued that the existence of outside shareholders will provide a more powerful force for efficiency and wise investment than the Treasury could ever achieve. That does, however, depend on shareholders being allowed to retain greater profits if the corporation is more efficient, which in turn depends on prices not being tied exclusively to costs. In the case of British Telecom, prices for the bulk of its services are tied to a figure 3 per cent below the Retail Price Index for the first five years. But it is difficult to see how, in the longer term, the regulatory authority Oftel will be able to determine prices so that Telecom's profits reflect its efficiency when there are no serious competitors with whom its costs can be compared.

One area where privatisation is certain to have some impact, however, is in the degree of detailed control which the Government of the day is able to exercise over the privatised companies. Buttressed by their private share-holders, insulated by semi-independent regulatory bodies, their Boards will be less susceptible to Government pressure over issues such as pricing policy, purchasing policy, labour relations, investments and closures. It is a matter of political perspective whether one sees this as an advantage or not. A Government dedicated to an interventionist industrial policy, believing that nationalisation can be used to build up key industries, support regional economies, protect the weaker sections of the public and ensure good conditions for the workers, would clearly regard it as a great loss. To someone who sees the interventions of past Governments as short-sighted responses to sectional interests and pressure groups, it is obviously a gain. And to those who share neither view in full, but see some sense in both points of view, the logical view would be to take each service, or each industry, on its own merits.

Turning to privatisation in the form of contracting-out of public services, the issues are rather different. John Rentoul presents a number of arguments. He points to loss of jobs and worsening conditions of service. Here, too, political perspective is crucial – a productivity gain to one individual is the loss of employment opportunity to another. Where one person sees privatisation leading to realistic, market-related wage rates, the other sees exploitation. He also criticises the proposed Bill (now postponed) which would have forced councils to put a number of services out to tender on the grounds, amongst others, that it would reduce councils to mere agents of Central Government. This is an issue which ranges far wider than the debate about privatisation – but he raises other issues which are central to the debate and which go beyond the particular proposals which have now been shelved.

He raises the question of how councils can reassure themselves that contractors will provide adequate levels of service. He cites the example of refuse collection, and reminds us of the 1963 Inquiry appointed by Sir Alec Douglas-Home (as he then was), which said that 'local authorities should not employ contractors to collect household refuse'.* And he quotes a former chief executive of the Kensington local authority on the subject in 1897: 'It was in the interests of the contractors to do as little as possible, and so increase their profits.'

He also questions the reality of any savings, pointing to the limited competition among contractors, their need to make a profit over and above their costs, and the costs to the local authorities of administering the contracted-out services.

The issue of contracting-out, of course, is not only restricted to the State. Private companies continually assess whether to make components or provide services in-house or, instead, whether to buy them in. Most of the issues raised by John Rentoul seem as relevant to them as they do to local authorities. In many cases where companies do contract-out crucial activities, they take care to foster good relations with their suppliers, who know they have to keep their customers satisfied. Often, companies will contract-out part of the activity so that there is less risk of being exploited by their

---

* 'Refuse Storage and Collection', Department of the Environment, 1967.

suppliers, and so that their own direct labour organisation is forced to compete and adapt in order to survive. But one precondition for the contracting-out solution to work properly is that both the contractor and the local authority should want it to work. This ingredient is missing in the current climate, where the Government seems to be ready to force local authorities to privatise key services.

Conclusion

Privatisation raises high passions. It goes to the heart of many of the political differences which divide the country. It is political, too, in a different sense, since it directly affects the distribution of power in the country. Privatisation greatly weakens the power of politicians, civil servants and trades unions in the nationalised industries and in the local authorities. By bringing in the force of the market, it adds to the power of those who already wield a great deal of it in industry and in the financial world. Nor is the argument of wider share-ownership entirely convincing, since the vast majority of shares end up in institutional hands.

In the argument both sides use and misuse evidence as the drunkard uses a lamp-post, for support rather than illumination. In any case, much of the evidence – on job losses, pay cuts, rationalisations or reductions in Government control – can be interpreted to support either side or neither.

Yet the debate is useful. The voter is entitled to consider the arguments put by those who feel strongly, and those who feel that the debate is too polarised and should be much more specific. Is privatisation the path to an efficient and economically bright future? Is the answer social ownership? Or can efficiency be achieved no matter who is running a service or an industry, and should we therefore be looking for participation by workers?